Living By Faith, Not By Feelings

Sickness, Surgery, Suffering and

Sorrow as a Person of Faith

31-Day Devotional

Dale Funderburg

ISBN 978-1-63903-271-6 (paperback)
ISBN 978-1-63903-272-3 (digital)

Christian Faith Publishing, Inc.
832 Park Avenue
Meadville, PA 16335
www.christianfaithpublishing.com

Printed in the United States of America

Introduction

Do all things without grumbling or disputing;
so that you will prove yourselves to be blameless
and innocent, children of God above reproach
in the midst of a crooked and perverse
generation, among whom you appear as lights in
the world, holding fast the word of life, so that
in the day of Christ I will have reason to glory
because I did not run in vain nor toil in vain.

—Philippians 2:14–16

DID YOU ENJOY LIVER AND ONIONS when you were a child? Me neither! My mother was an excellent traditional southern cook. She tried to cook liver only once that I recall, southern-fried, battered, and smothered in brown gravy. She tried to pass it off as "minute" steak, a family favorite. Well, it didn't take a minute for her ruse to fall apart. I took one bite and immediately looked to my older sister for guidance. She was already staring wide-eyed back at me. Using our best sibling telepathy, we asked each other without saying it out loud, *What are we going to do?* We didn't want to hurt Mama's feelings. But the more I chewed, the bigger the bite grew inside my mouth. It was not the taste only; it was also a texture "thang." That had to violate some natural law of physics or digestive health or something! Thankfully, my mother took one bite, discreetly eased it back out into her napkin, and graciously said, "I think I'll make some biscuits." It was years before we ever spoke about what became known as the liver incident. I think my Daddy buried it deep outside the fence for fear the dog might dig it up. And we loved our dog.

The process of writing the pages that follow has been the same experience—the more I chewed on it, the bigger the bite became. (Although I do hope you find the flavor of what I've penned a little tastier than the liver. I hope as well the following pages do not end up in a shallow grave).

The idea that gave birth to the pages that follow started as a suggestion from a speech therapist in the Methodist hospital in Memphis, Tennessee. After enduring so much physical trauma and being put to sleep several times in such a short period and experiencing what the hospital staff referred to as a near-death experience, I was having difficulty speaking the words which my brain intended. I couldn't connect my thoughts with my tongue. I have seen the same frustrating situation with stroke victims. Being a pastor, preaching and public speaking is a huge part of my life, so to say I was concerned is an understatement. The speech therapist suggested writing a journal of the events that led up to that moment. So this project started as a mere exercise to help my brain and body to make up and play nice together again. However, the more I wrote, and then independently, the more I prayed and tried to make sense of all that was happening to me physically, the Lord revealed He had a higher purpose for what I was putting down on paper.

I have a family, a church family, friends, and an entire community that prayed for me through my darkest hours. Some of the events were so fluid there was no time to send details, but the need for immediate intercession was critical. Thus, several times during the ordeal, there was little more information than could be contained in text messages. Yet people prayed fervently and effectually. I now feel those folks deserve to know what happened and how God answered prayers and intervened on my behalf. What a mighty God we serve!

As I completed writing "My Story" in chronological order of the events, I did not feel it was a finished product. I hoped the account of my medical drama might encourage people enduring similar frustrating and frightening medical situations. I also would hope this record can serve those who are in the business of giving medical care. It can hopefully be a gracious record of how most laypeople feel when we are horizontally challenged and confined to a hospital bed. I hope "My Story" is an encouragement for those dealing with medical issues to hear what God has done for me and take heart. I hope it is a reminder that when we enjoy health, we should always show compassion. For the patient and their family and friends, I hope "My Story" can encourage them to have faith, trusting God will be the one to use the hospital staff as instruments in His hand.

The following account is also for the gifted professional. Please remember, as you provide care, it is to people who are uncertain and maybe a bit afraid. Your explanations and medical knowledge give us confidence. Your bedside manner and attitude and compassion provide us with comfort. We need both!

However, there is a higher purpose in writing this journal and devotional. As Paul said, I do not want to have "*run in vain nor toil in vain*" (Galatians 2:2, Galatians 3:4). I have been confirmed personally in my faith. I hope to reveal in the following pages, "My Story" is living proof that Romans 8:28 is still valid, "*And we know that God causes all things to work together for good to those who love God, to those who are called according to His purpose.*" It is also my hope that my "running" and "toiling" can glorify God and encourage the discipleship of fellow Believers.

God is still on His throne, and He is still sovereign, even when everything else seems out of control. It is to fulfill this higher purpose where "My Story" becomes "Our Story." There is not a single incident in my experience of which I now write that I did not seek to apply biblical principles to seek to learn a more profound lesson. "My Story" is unique to me, and I hope never to have a repeat performance. However, there are biblical truths and life principles that can be seen in the shadows, working behind every situation.

I have divided the stories into short devotionals to tie them together. It is my prayer that anyone facing medically challenging situations and their families can read "My Story" and find comfort. I hope it can be a lighthearted distraction from how terrifyingly overwhelming medical drama can feel. I hope through "Our Story," those same people and the people who care for them can find more than comfort. I hope you will discover the hope found in the right and perfect will of a good and gracious God.

There are practical and genuine reasons to note: there were overwhelming medical reasons for everyone in the operating room to believe that "My Story" almost came to an end. An open incision in the lumbar region of my back exposing a ruptured spinal cord losing spinal fluid is severe enough. The process to surgically repair my spinal cord was interrupted by a massive heart attack, a lost pulse, a Code Blue, and chaos. All of this happening at the same time is any surgical team's worst nightmare. Patched together just enough to turn me over, to attempt to revive me, and then for it not to happen without multiple attempts caused some to prepare themselves for the worst. Of course, I survived. When the medical team later told me what had happened, there was a peace that attended my soul, so much so that some of the medical professionals did not believe I grasped the severity of the situation. But I did.

It seems a bit pious for me to compare my medical condition to Paul's persecution for the sake of the Gospel. I am not comparing hardships, but I am claiming the faith that gave me peace gave Paul the perspective to write "for me to live is Christ; to die is gain" (Philippians 1:21). I have never been more assured of my salvation than during the moments contained in the pages that follow. Never have I had so much confidence that when death does come for me, it will have no sting. Don't get me wrong! I hope to live a long and meaningful and fruitful life, but I face life with much less wonder about death. The confidence I have now has nothing to do with me, nor my experiences. It has everything to do with abiding in Christ. I feel inadequate to describe it, but I'm in good company. Paul identified it as *"peace that passes understanding"* (Philippians 1:21). In the powerful hymn of Horatio Spafford, I can declare, *"Whatever my lot, thou hast taught me to say / It is well, it is well, with my soul."*

— ❧ —

Day 1

Trusting God...with the Details of Life

Trust in the Lord with all your heart and
do not lean on your own understanding.
In all your ways acknowledge Him, and
He will make your paths straight.

—Proverbs 3:5–6

I BELIEVE IN THE SOVEREIGNTY OF God unapologetically. I don't understand precisely how every experience of life fits into His plan, but I trust Him. As kids, my cousin Sherry loved to put puzzles together. I appreciated the finished product, but putting all those little pieces together was not my idea of fun, nor did it feel like a stress reliever—just the opposite. I might even have been guilty of forcing a piece to fit where it wasn't supposed to fit. Making one piece fit also meant there was another piece that wasn't supposed to fit at another spot, so I forced it also. What should be a beautiful picture of a barn and field and farm critters turned into a picture of a barn with a cow on the roof and a weather vane with an otter on my puzzle.

I am still learning to trust God with the pieces of my life. I have no problem believing that eternity or heaven or the vast universe or a zillion other mountain-range-size truths are more than I can fully comprehend. I rest in the faith that all of those things are the Almighty's department and above my pay grade. I learn a little more as I age, but it should be enough for this simple man to be left speechless and in *awe* about many things. However, I'm embarrassed to say that at the little speed bumps of life, my slack jaw of amazement turns to a frown, and the raised eyebrows of my wonder become furrowed at difficulties. Those are times in which I'm guilty of trying to make the pieces fit where I want them instead of trusting God with the little details. My attitude often goes from awe to awful. The booming voice of my praise to God turns to the sniffling whine of Nellie Olsen from *Little House on the Prairie*. I'm ashamed of how quickly I can go from lifting my eyes, looking upward toward the eastern sky to the tunnel vision of weakness and frailty.

August 17, 2019, is one of the little pieces of the puzzle of my story. I was checking on the baptistery on that Saturday night in preparation for the Sunday morning worship service. Two steps down to the control panel, and a big sneeze sent my size 13 EEE out and up, and I landed on the steps, directly on the small of my back. Although I was all alone, I jumped up and looked around to shrug it off pridefully, just in case there might be a witness. I was raised to believe, if a man wants to gain membership into the macho-redneck-real-men-don't-cry fraternity, he could not acknowledge pain. If you are injured, you better not rub it! When I realized there was no one to see me or to be embarrassed in front of, I was quickly transported to memories of being a five-year-old first grader in Mrs. Thompson's class without the sophisticated skills of hiding shame. Most people describe a fall or hard hit as getting the wind knocked out of them. Pardon my crudeness, but my fall involved more about my bladder than my lungs!

Our story: living by grace

Life is full of uncertainty and instability. Schedules and structure may help as tools for administration and organization, but they only provide a false sense of security that is not real. Most people are comforted when there is a regularity to life. However, when tragedy does strike, uncertainty becomes all the more dramatic. Stress and fear surround the traumatic events, only to enhance uncertainty and instability. It becomes a vicious cycle.

The believer is not immune to tragedy because it is merely part of life. Adam and Eve sinned, and the resulting depravity has touched every part of my life. However, I've been redeemed, and every part of my life has also been affected by the grace of God. I may not know when tragedy or difficulties will interrupt my life. Nonetheless, whatever I face, I will not face it alone because I walk with God and He with me. Jesus is included in my schedule and the structure of my everyday life. Therefore, when life is good, it's because He is there with me. I praise and thank Him and celebrate His blessings. When life becomes hard, I pray and trust Him, and I am comforted because He is there with me also. Walking with God is possible by grace and is the key to assurance. There is always the possibility for a sneeze and a fall just around the corner. There is also the promise that whether walking or slipping, Jesus is there with me. I want to glorify Him through my attitude and action as well as my response and reaction.

Genesis 5 contains a list of the descendants of Adam. Verses 21–24 focus on a man named Enoch. It says that Enoch *"walked with God and was no more, for God took him."* We know Adam sinned and was expelled from the garden. It is known as the Fall of Man because that nature of sin was handed down to every person since Adam, except one. We know the only hope whereby we can be right with God is through a relationship of faith in that one sinless man: Jesus, by trusting His finished work. We are sinners like the first Adam, a truth that applied to Enoch too. So how was Enoch saved? He was saved the same way Noah was saved in Genesis 6:8, *"Noah found grace in the eyes of the Lord."* He was saved the same way we can be saved—by grace (Ephesians 2:8–9). The point is, Enoch was not saved *because* he walked with God. Enoch believed and was saved *in order to* walk with God. We are given a clear picture in Hebrews 11, the great hall of fame of faith. Verses 5–6 tell us, *"By faith, Enoch was taken up so that he would not see death; and he was not found because God took him up; for he obtained the witness that before his being taken up he was pleasing to God. And without faith, it is impossible to please*

9

Him, for he who comes to God must believe that He is and that He is a rewarder of those who seek Him."

So how can we please God? By faith! It is not a matter of our feelings or comfort or prosperity. Today, live because Christ is *in* you, and you are *in* Christ. Walk by faith, choosing to obey God's word, seeking Him in the moment. Trust God with the details of your day, then you too, by faith, can "walk with God."

— ❧ —

My Story

Day 2

Being Afraid...
but Not Fearful

Peace I leave with you; My peace I give to you;
not as the world gives do I give to you. Do not
let your heart be troubled, nor let it be fearful.

—John 14:27

I KNEW MY BACK WAS HURT more than my feelings, but I decided to tough it out. My concern grew less about my back and more about my bladder. My outlook on life is usually a glass-half-full kind of guy. However, after the fall, my perspective became more focused on a bladder-always-full type of guy. I knew something was wrong, but with my fifty-ninth birthday around the corner, I figured it was something to do with the fall of Adam more than the fall of Dale. Adam chose to sin, and the result affected everything about this world, including sickness, sorrow, death as we know it, including fifty-eight-year-old men's bladders. I also thought the weird pain in my right leg would surely get better with time, like cheese or wine, but I was "whining" about it anyway. Fast-forward another week before I saw the doctor, and as a result, I found myself inside an MRI machine. By the way, MRI stands for "*Maximum Reality* that *I* need up out dis coffin."

As a man who stands six foot five and weighs in at two hundred and plenty, I am also claustrophobic. As a small child, I thought how fun it would be to follow my older cousin into a culvert to crawl under the road. Not the best idea. When that childhood fear resurfaces as an adult, I will rearrange some furniture to find relief. But now, by the doctor's orders, I am expected to suppress that response and voluntarily go inside a medical machine not much bigger than that culvert. The problem is, I am much bigger now. The MRI is an innovative technology and a tool that features the marvel of modern medical imaging. For me, it is more like a cannon at the circus, and I was praying for somebody to light the fuse. Once inside, I confessed sins I haven't even committed and employed the familiar bargaining tactics we all sometimes resort to in a moment of weakness. God demonstrated His sense of humor when the technician's voice declared she was moving me out but for me to remain still. I would be free. Oh, the joy to feel the one-foot table on which my two-foot shoulders balanced and wedged inside an eighteen-inch chamber was actually moving me out at the speed of smell; but it was moving me out. Glory! Free at last; free at last...but freedom was short-lived. I was told not to move because "We're not finished." Then this charming, sweet hero that had freed me from the chamber of torture suddenly turned green with a broom in hand, and a flying monkey peeking over her shoulder told me this was an MRI "with contrast." She said, "You have to go back in...and your little dog too." I wished for some size 13 EEE ruby slippers to rapture me away.

If you are unfamiliar with medical jargon, allow me to explain the experience of an "MRI with contrast." "With contrast" means they stick a needle the size of a twenty-penny nail in your vein and pump pepper sauce into your circulatory system. You learn in a unique way where critical organs are located by feeling Tabasco run through your body, highlighting where your kidneys, heart, and other innards are, and then you go back inside the coffin. My mama taught me never to hit a girl, and I never did, except my sister... once. Although I must admit, at that moment, all sorts of options ran through my mind. Grace and better judgment prevailed. I did survive, and no one had to file charges.

Our story: living by grace

Every believer will go through experiences we dread; some even elicit the "fight or flight" emotional responses. There may be those experiences that shake our bones to the tune of a good knee knocking. However, the experiences do not sway our faith. Hebrews 10:31 says, "*It is a terrifying thing to fall into the hands of the living God.*" Every day should be filled with *awe* of God. However, in our culture, there is very little left to the imagination of how evil and dangerous our world has become. The twenty-four-hour news cycle replays horrors and hopelessness from around the globe. Politicians hate each other. Science has dismissed God from anything other than religion. And too many are in the religion "business," instead of Gospel calling. How difficult would it be for an honest assessment of our culture to be boiled down to two words found in Revelation 21:8: "*the fearful and unbelieving.*"

As believers, we find forgiveness and comfort through faith. By faith, we hold Christ's hand daily, even in experiences that upset us. We may not understand all the dynamics of this life, but we know we can trust the hand we hold because it is nail-scarred with His love for us. Romans 5:8 says, "*God demonstrates His own love toward us, in that while we were yet sinners, Christ died for us.*" We have assurance and confidence because of the love Christ demonstrated toward us. Romans 8 goes to great lengths to build within us an understanding that nothing can separate us from that love. When we listen to the other voice of our condemnation, then fear takes over, accompanied by doubt and shame, which lend themselves back to fear.

Fear is a weapon our enemy will use to attack the most seasoned disciple of Christ. Our fear, linked to our sinful nature, is to believe, somehow, we will be exposed in our unworthiness before God. This fear is unreasonable as if God does not already know our vulnerabilities. It's the same lie that made Adam hide from God in Eden. However, the lonely condition of our greatest need can also hold the key to unlock faith too. The lie behind our greatest fear is that of losing control. The temptation for Eve was wanting to "become like God, knowing good and evil." Now culture calls for people to take

13

control of their lives. The idea that we are the masters of the universe empowers men. It becomes the rationale to overcome addiction, to correct the direction of one's life, to demand equality in relationships, and a host of other issues. But is that actually a tangible reality: to take control of my life? Jesus calls us to something very different. He calls us to abandon the pursuits to control our life by surrendering to Him as the object of our faith. In Luke 9:23, Jesus says, "*Whoever wants to be my disciple must deny themselves and take up their cross daily and follow me.*"

Fear manipulates us. Faith frees us. Fear calls us to run away. Faith calls us to run to Christ. Fear causes restlessness. Faith brings peace that passes understanding. The disciples all ran away from the garden of Gethsemane and hid because of their fear. Later, they experienced changed lives. They all became willing to face the most atrocious threats and horrifying deaths bravely. What changed? What happened? The cross and the empty tomb are what happened. The Gospel message became much more than words for each of them. They believed. They learned to take up their cross daily to follow Jesus…all the way to *glory*!

My Story

Day 3

Trusting God...Even in Uncertainty

And they that know thy name will put
their trust in thee: for thou, Lord, hast
not forsaken them that seek thee.

—Psalm 9:10

AFTER SPENDING ALL DAY IN WAITING rooms, doing paperwork, talking to insurance clerks, answering the same questions, sometimes to the same people, an entire four whole minutes with the doctor and the longest forty-five minutes on record in a torture chamber, I was finally walking through the parking lot to get to my truck. (If you know me, then you know parking lots hold a different fearful recurring nightmare, but that's another story). My phone rang. It was my doctor's nurse, insisting I return to his office. Driving over, I questioned myself, *Did I forget to pay my copay?*

When I walked into the building, there was no sign-in or waiting rooms; the nurse met me at the door. We didn't go to an exam room. We met the doctor in his office, and he sat me in front of his computer screen. He already had the results of the MRI. Really? I still had a nervous twitch from the pictures being made, and he already had the results? Technology! He pointed to the screen, and I remember thinking that it needed cleaning. On the picture in front of me was an image resembling a black-and-white aerial view from Google Earth, focused miles above the Becker Bottom. However, it turned out to be a lateral image of my backbone. As he pointed out the lumbar region, he rolled the arrow across what he identified as L1, L2, and L3. He outlined the spinal cord, and I immediately observed the screen was really dirty at those places. I thought, *Man, somebody should clean that screen because if I didn't know better, I'd think that big old spot was a part of the MRI image.* Then I realized the screen was clean.

The doctor told me I had a tumor. He said it was an intradural tumor, meaning it was inside of my spinal cord. It had most of the nerves from L2 down blocked off into a thin ribbon. The fall in the baptistry did not cause this tumor, but the fall did make it symptomatic. The urgency of my bladder issues was severe, and the damage could be permanent. The pain in my right leg was schizophrenic. One moment it was burning; the next moment, it was numb and tingling. The worst sensation was the Tasmanian devil trying to escape down the back of my leg and out of my big toe. The tumor would have to be surgically removed by a neurosurgeon or risk permanent nerve damage and even possible paralysis. Honestly, I didn't comprehend much past the word *tumor.* All my inner monologue could focus on was the voice of Arnold Schwarzenegger from *Kindergarten Cop,* saying, "It is not a tu-mor." But it was.

I was trying to convince myself that my bladder issues and the pain in my leg were due to the fall and birthdays. Anybody would hurt after that kind of fall. I don't know how to "rub some dirt on it" for your bladder, but that was my attitude. Give it a little time, and it will be better. Hold your chin up, be tough, push through. And the place I had most confidence: trust God. And now it looked as if God was placing me in the hands of people who knew how to do more than rub some dirt on it.

Our story: living by grace

No reasonable adult ever expects an infant to act like a teenager. It is natural for a baby to have no sense of control over their response to their needs. That's why Pampers makes a fortune! It is why babies cry when they are hungry, wet, dirty, sleepy, and sometimes just want to be held. However, when the same child grows to be a teenager, everyone expects him to know how to be disciplined, to control his responses to most of their needs. The cycle of the stages of life and the corresponding expectation of maturity continues until we die, or we decline due to the thieves of dementia or Alzheimer's robbing us of memories and control. We laugh with joy while we feed a baby. We fight back the tears when we put the bib on our parents.

All of our lives, we deal with our emotions, our discipline, and our responses, none of which can sustain us. From the moment we're born until the moment we die, we battle our fleshly selfishness and the cultural influences to conform. The only hope any of us hold is to *not* live by our emotions, fear, or happiness but by faith in Christ. Faith is not only an emotional response; it is the surrender of who we are to Christ. It is believing that <u>He</u> is where we find forgiveness as well as fulfillment. It is faith that sees us through uncertainty. It is by faith we overcome in this life and, with certainty, in eternity. First John 5:4–5 says, *"For whatever is born of God overcomes the world; and this is the victory that has overcome the world: our faith. And who is the one who overcomes the world, but he who believes that Jesus is the Son of God."*

Romans 12:2 instructs us, *"Do not be conformed to this world, but be transformed by the renewing of your mind, so that you may prove what the will of God is, that which is good and acceptable and perfect."* Far too often, we focus on the negative of the instruction, *"do not be conformed to this world."* Our emphasis can quickly become about what we should *not* do. After all, the majority of the ten commandments start with *"Thou shalt not."* However, genuine repentance means turning *from* our sin but also means we turn *to* Christ. Authentic discipleship focuses more on the positive—*"be transformed"*—which happens by *"the renewing of your mind."*

Transformation is a process. Renewal is more than a statement; it involves change. Transformation, renewal, and change often include pain. However, when the work of change is mature, the result will disarm doubt because the child of God can *"prove what the will of God is."* When doubt is not the default for the soul, then fear is replaced by confidence, not in yourself but God's faithfulness. The transformational process of renewing your mind daily in God's word hides little nuggets of truth in the heart that resurface at just the appropriate moment. Hebrews 4:12 declares the *"word of God is living and active."* Indeed, we hide God's word in our heart to keep us from sin (Psalm 119:11) but also to quiet our soul when every other voice shouts the evidence of pain, fear, shame, loss, and defeat. The mind renewed daily in the living and active word of God has no reason to panic. If you learn to drive on a farm, then you probably learn how to back up first, perhaps backing a trailer. Maybe it might be helpful to understand Romans 12:2 if you back into it too. By faith, we know that God's will is "perfect," "acceptable," and "good." But how do you "prove what the will of God is"? By the "renewing of your mind" by being "transformed." Herein lies the secret of Psalm 46:10, *"Be still, and know that I am God."*

— ✤ —

My Story

Day 4

Trusting God...
Needing Prayer

Bear one another's burdens, and
thereby fulfill the law of Christ.

—Galatians 6:2

AFTER RECEIVING THE NEWS OF THE tumor, I went home and told my wife. The first thing we did was to pray for healing and/or peace and wisdom. Then we called our kids. I told my sister Donna but withheld the news from Judy, my oldest sister. I did not tell her initially, partly because I didn't want to read about it in her post on Facebook but because she was a worrier. I would wait until just before the surgery to tell Judy. LeeAnn shared the news with her sisters. I told our church staff because they are my friends and prayer partners, but also they were going to be the ones to help make it through this long-term daily process and how it affected our church family. We told this handful of people to pray, but otherwise, we were going to keep it close to the vest until we had more answers and learned more details.

The next Sunday, I greeted a sweet, faithful saint who responded, "My, oh my! To have undergone surgery this week, you are surely looking good!" Not five minutes later, another concerned soul asked, "Did they get it all? Have you started treatments? You look good."

Not much of an ego booster to know I look good for a man who supposedly had surgery and started treatments inside a week. I decided that at the end of the morning worship service, I would tell the church family what I knew. My motive behind the report was (1) I value the prayers of Godly people and (2) the way "prayer requests" sometimes are enhanced, I feared the grapevine would have me buried before evening Bible study.

Our story: living by grace

First John 4 makes it clear *why* and *how* we can love each other, *"Beloved, if God so loved us, we also ought to love one another."* John 13:34–35 is clear; one of the results of loving each other is *"by this shall all men know that you are my disciples, if you have love one to another."* If we love through Christ, what could be more natural than to pray for each other? James 5:16 is a beautiful picture of believers fulfilling "all things new." It says, *"Confess your faults one to another, and pray one for another, that you may be healed. The effectual fervent prayer of a righteous man availeth much."*

It encourages me and humbles me to know people pray for their pastor every day. It comforts me to know I can ask for prayer and have confidence, not only that God hears prayer but that "righteous" men and women participate to pray for me. The reason "My Story" even continues is because of "Our Story" in prayer. The reason I am healed through the circumstances of which I write is that *my* God hears prayers of righteous men and women and students and children who got involved and networked with each other but, more importantly with heaven in effectual and fervent prayer. Do not take the privilege of praying for each other lightly. Let your prayers be extravagant, not about your *wants* but about the needs in your life and the needs around you. Let your prayer be out of control. Do not only pray for a proverbial parking place to protect your life from getting a mark from someone else's door. Pray hard enough to cost you something: effectually and fervently. Pray hard enough to involve the body of Christ and *your* body *in* Christ. Pray so hard your knees buckle in humility and empathy. Pray so fervently that your hand reaches for the hurting to comfort. Pray so hard your eyes water in sympathy. Pray so hard your voice will quiver, and your brain will search because you do not quite have the words adequate to express the groanings your heart demands.

John 10:10 is the outing of the devil's strategy, "*The thief comes but to steal and kill and destroy.*" The devil does not want you to be a "righteous" person in Christ. But if you are a blood-bought child of God, in Christ alone, through faith alone, the devil is impotent to subvert grace. However, he can steal, kill, and destroy the effect of your righteousness, if you allow him. He is a "*roaring lion seeking whom he may devour.*" He uses every "*fiery arrow*" as the "*accuser of the brethren*" to lie as the "*father of lies*" to deceive you into believing that your prayers do not mean anything. But if you're reading what I'm writing, then the lie is exposed. The word of our testimony has silenced the accuser; the arrow is extinguished, and the lion is caged—prayer "availeth" much. The devil is defeated *not* because of my efforts (not the pray-ER). Victory comes because of the one to whom we pray! Those very words will show up again in "My Story" because I believe them to be true and give hope enough to live by them!

— ✤ —

My Story
Day 5

Trusting God...in Disappointment

The Lord is near to the brokenhearted and
saves those who are crushed in spirit.

—Psalm 34:18

MY MRI IMAGES AND OTHER RECORDS were forwarded to UAB in Birmingham. Wow! I began to sense the seriousness of my medical condition. UAB was one of the gold standard research and specialty hospitals in the south. It's the place where they airlift the worst to get the best. People are taken to UAB to get well. It is huge! When I visit UAB as a pastor, I find out which building I'm visiting. Otherwise, a fellow could walk a couple of miles in downtown Birmingham around eight or nine blocks. We waited another week like a kid at a country church homecoming dinner—on the grounds in line for a one-seat outhouse...and remember, I was having bladder issues! A week seemed like a month. The news I received shook my soul a bit. UAB declined to take my case. The people around me in the medical field tried to comfort me by saying that's no biggie. I would smile in response, but it was big...and terrifying and dramatic in my mind. Were doctors at UAB saying there's no hope? Surely there had to be at least one doctor in the plethora of experts who had popped the hood on a case like mine. They later said it was about insurance, but for me, it was about assurance. I was terrified.

As I've said, I usually am a glass-half-full kind of guy. I try to look on the bright side. Honestly, I look for the humor in life, even on cloudy days. As a child, I felt most gratified when I made my mama laugh. I think it's a good thing if people can laugh, even at a funeral. I interpret Proverbs 17:22 literally, *"A merry heart does good like medicine,"* and there's no copay. Some people think it's inappropriate to smile or laugh in church. Do you know what my response is about those people? I laugh, but I'm also sad for them! Yes, I can even laugh at myself, and I don't mind if people laugh with me, but not at me. I can find humor in almost anything, but when I heard UAB said no, silence fell across my wit. I caught myself holding my breath. But within days, my doctor had an appointment for me with a neurosurgeon at the Semmes Murphey Clinic in Memphis. I had no experience, nor had I ever heard of Semmes Murphey. I soon learned they were the BMOC when it comes to the brain and spine. That's all they do at the Semmes Murphey Clinic—brain and spine. I felt a smile coming back across my soul.

Our story: living by grace

Fear is more than a response or reaction. Being fearful can become a frame of mind and an outlook on life. Numbers 13–14 tells an interesting story. The children of Israel sent twelve spies into the promised land to gain military insight about what they were to encounter if they were to conquer this land of promise. Two of the dozen reported about what they *saw*, and the other ten reported about what they *feared*. Ten of them said, "Oh, yeah, it's a land flowing with great things, but listen to us—there are giants there that are way too big for us to hit!" Joshua and Caleb's attitudes were the opposite: "What? No, those guys are too big to *miss*! We're going to take their lunch money if we just obey God!" The people believed that the majority rules, but it doesn't! God rules! Because the adults listened to their fear, they would not be part of the obedient faithful to possess the land. The ten spies and the grumbling generation who listened to them died before entering the promised land. However, Joshua and Caleb were spared and became leaders in claiming the promise because they did not succumb to peer pressure or allow their faith to be governed by their feelings based upon mere physical evidence. They were men who lived by faith! Caleb, at eighty-five years old, picked out which mountain he would claim by faith!

Second Peter 1:1–4 opens with these words:

> *Simon Peter, a bond-servant and apostle of Jesus Christ, To those who have received a faith of the same kind as ours, by the righteousness of our God and Savior, Jesus Christ: Grace and peace be multiplied to you in the knowledge of God and of Jesus our Lord; seeing that His divine power has granted to us everything pertaining to life and godliness, through the true knowledge of Him who called us by His own glory and excellence. For by these He has granted to us His precious and magnificent promises, so that by them you may become partakers of the divine nature, having escaped the corruption that is in the world by lust.*

We do not always know what lies around the corner, and our flesh might tell us to fear the unknown—there may be giants there. But faith *knows* who is around the corner for us, already there, waiting with all the protection and provision we will need—Jesus.

Edgar Allan Poe wrote some brilliant and weird stuff. In *The System of Dr. Tarr and Professor Fether*, the head of a private mental institution said, "Believe nothing you hear, and only half of what you see." That's how many people seem to live their lives concerning spirituality, especially in skeptical responses to biblical truth. However, the Bible says, *"Faith comes by hearing, and hearing by the Word of God"* (Romans 10:17). Your eyes will fool you. If you've ever been put to sleep, you can see some amazing things that are not real, but your family will enjoy your descriptions as you begin waking up! If you go through a divorce, you're going to see things differently through the pain. If you lose a loved one, you may see life differently through sorrow. That is why *"looking unto Jesus, the author and finisher of our faith"* (Hebrews 12:2) is truly the only reliable balance in all experiences of this life…and beyond. I am built to believe in something bigger than myself. My sinful pride wants to selfishly hold onto that claim that my universe orbits around me. Deep down, I know better. Christ becomes my "finisher of faith," which means He provides maturity and completion. He provides the answer to the question "What more is out there?" He calms all fears!

— ⚜ —

My Story

Day 6

Trusting God... through the Process

But David encouraged himself
in the Lord his God.

—1 Samuel 30:6

IN A MATTER OF WEEKS, I drove to my first appointment with Dr. Laverne R. Lovell at a branch office of the Semmes Murphey Clinic in Oxford, Mississippi. Their main office is in Memphis, Tennessee, but they have offices in Oxford, Southaven, Jackson, Tennessee, and Jonesboro, Arkansas. Several doctors are part of this group of specialists. I found out Semmes Murphey is world-renowned. They work closely with Methodist Hospital and Le Bonheur Children's Hospital, Baptist Hospital, as well as other top hospitals in the Memphis area. They have patients from all over the world coming to seek their help and find healing. Although it was hard for a Mississippi State fan to drive to Oxford, I was relieved to get the appointment so soon and not have to drive the round trip of 350 miles to Memphis and back home in a day.

A few days before the appointment, I received a call and was instructed to go online to sign up on their patient portal and fill out the profile. I did, but based on my experience with other medical professionals, I wondered how many times I'd fill out the same information. I've considered, at times, answering some of those routine questions with obviously wrong answers, just to see if they read it. But the risk of being scheduled for a mammogram or worse has usually held my warped sense of humor at bay. Although I will admit that I have designated my height as five feet seventeen inches several times, and I've yet to be confronted. Upon arriving for my appointment, there was a single page to fill out, and before I could even finish it, I was being summoned to come back to an examination room. I asked myself, *Am I in the right place?* Usually, you determine they have named the waiting room very appropriately. A visit to the doctor often means a wait time long enough to at least read through the books of the Pauline letters in the New Testament. I've sat in waiting rooms long enough to make it through the book of Leviticus, while even making notes. On this day, I couldn't have read the short single-chapter book of Jude in the waiting room before they called me back! Many clinics now have the outer waiting room and a smaller inner waiting room, the station to have blood pressure checked, a line of seats in the hall and, finally, the exam room. I'm waiting for them to put the zigzag lines like the amusement parks in the parking lot. I've also noticed many clinics have a place for you to pay upfront as the first point of entry and then another place to pay after the visit so you can pay again. Either they are hoping with all the waiting that it has been so long you forgot you paid an entrance fee, or they've run so many tests that you've got to establish monthly installments higher than a car payment.

Our story: living by grace

One of the most dangerous times as a Christian is when we have idle minds and idle hands because we are waiting for an event or an appointment. None of us like to wait. I have the oil in my truck changed every three thousand miles. I go to the dentist for regular cleanings and checkups. I go to the doctor when I'm sick but also for routine checkups. These days, I seem to be going to a lot of doctors. As a pastor, people make appointments, and often they arrive late.

Five minutes here, ten minutes there, and thirty minutes over and over add up. LeeAnn and I have three children that are all grown now. Before the kids came along, I was a married young man who had not yet learned how to calculate that when my young bride said she would be ready in twenty minutes, it actually was on "makeup and hairspray savings time," which meant to set your clock back one hour. The point I'm making is I've learned how to wait without it becoming idle and useless time. Waiting rooms can be a field *"white unto harvest."* I cannot recount the number of times that a casual conversation has turned into a divine appointment to enter into a Gospel conversation. Waiting for an oil change may cross my path with people who would never come listen to a sermon, but they are ready to talk when they find someone willing to listen to them. A ride to visit someone in the hospital in Tupelo is a two-hour round trip—an excellent time to pray, to meditate on Scripture, or even be quiet and still to listen to God. I rarely turn on the radio.

David had been anointed king a long time before he took the throne. He even got chased around by Saul. He sat inside a few caves hiding out during those days. First Samuel 30:6 says, *"But David encouraged himself in the Lord his God."* There are moments we need to be active and physically busy to do our Father's will. But there are times to be still. There is much comfort to simply be "abiding" in Him. In John 15, Jesus said, *"I am the vine, you are the branches; he who abides in Me and I in him, he bears much fruit, for apart from Me you can do nothing.... My Father is glorified by this, that you bear much fruit, and so prove to be My disciples"* (John 15:5, 8). Abiding *in* Him gives great confidence, and Christ abiding *in* me provides great comfort. There is no path in this life that I'll walk alone. And when we remember our job is to be the branch, not the vine, then we can allow the Holy Spirit to put the words in our mouth; like the vine supplies the branches, the fruit is the result of that life-giving nutrition from the vine.

Abiding is a picture of active resting. But we will not live in this world forever. The world will not last forever. Jesus will return. In Luke 12, Jesus shares a parable about men waiting on their Lord. The passage contains an implicit warning to my heart. Jesus will return, and I want to be ready and watching and waiting.

—— ✣ ——

My Story

Day 7

Trusting God...and People Who Trust God

Bear one another's burdens, and
thereby fulfill the law of Christ.

—Galatians 6:12

AFTER THE ROUTINE CHECKING OF MY temperature, blood pressure, and pleasantries with a friendly staff, Dr. Lovell came into the room. Dr. Lovell is a very distinguished man. Older than I, but not by much. He was a fit man with a slim build. And most importantly, he was not looking at a chart when he walked into the exam room. He looked me in the eye, introduced himself, and shook my hand. I had already read his bio on their website. He retired from the military before Semmes Murphey sought him out to join their group of neurosurgeons. That information alone registers great respect for me personally. I admire and feel indebted to all who serve in our military. However, it did not take long after meeting the man that his genuine concern for me was calming and comforting. He is a very personable man. We talked about what brought me to this visit, and Dr. Lovell, although already thoroughly knowledgeable about my circumstances and test results, wanted to hear from me. He listened. What a great lesson for every professional who deals with people to learn. No matter if you are a physician, plumber, probation officer, or pastor, people need to know we care. We are first of all a person, and anyone with whom we are dealing is also a person. Many times, that person needs more than surgery, service, or counsel. They need to know they are important to us. Sometimes the greatest gift we can give is a moment of undivided attention. How can a business person advance by paying such attention to detail about his job but not know the importance of listening to his wife and children? How can a mother be so attentive to the slightest whimper of her newborn baby but lose sight that the same child as a teenager or young adult needs to have his or her mother's ear as well as her heart? I've been blessed to have good relationships with our family doctors through the years, but I've also been a chart number who needed a diagnosis. Care of the soul is essential too. Dr. Lovell proved to be a doctor who understands that truth.

Dr. Lovell carried me from the exam room to his office and sat me in front of his computer with the same familiar MRI image displayed. He delivered the same diagnosis about the tumor and the reality that it must be removed. He told me this was a very rare tumor. I already knew that. I had read that of all tumors, the chance of having one like mine was about one-half of 1 percent. Yes, I made the mistake of consulting with the internet, even watching YouTube videos of surgeries of removing the same kind of tumor.

Having hope of healing but then consulting the internet holds sort of a strange ironic and paradoxical trauma for the patient's outlook. It is kind of like a man I once knew who neutered his aggressive dog, which is not necessarily uncommon on the farm. However, a few days later, he ran over the same dog. The real irony is the dog was named Lucky. Consulting Google is *not* the place to seek comfort before surgery. However, it is so hard not to go there because we want information. It could be compared to driving by a wreck on the highway; you can't help but look! However, Dr. Lovell assured me that he had done many of these same types of surgeries, and he was almost certainly sure that the tumor was benign, and that I would be healed. Then he said something that brought me the greatest comfort. It was not forced. It was as natural as his diagnosis. He said he would do his part as a neurosurgeon, but it was most important to know God would do His part. I do not believe he only said that because I am a pastor. He said it so naturally that I believed that *he* believed it—what a wonderful gift of comfort and confidence. For the first time in several weeks, I saw a light at the end of the tunnel, and I was not afraid it was a train!

Our story: living by grace

One of the most significant benefits of being part of a local family of faith is when you have a burden, you have someone to help bear that burden. Such is the ministry behind the command of Galatians 6:12, "*Bear one another's burdens, and thereby fulfill the law of Christ.*" When I lifted weights, if I were trying to push myself, I'd make sure I had a spotter—someone there to help if the weight became too much. It is our natural prideful flesh that will not accept that kind of help. If someone helping us bear the burden fulfills the law of Christ, then where does that leave us if we refuse the help? No person doesn't need help, only those who are too prideful to admit it. Some things are not designed to be experienced alone. Sawing a log with a double-handled crosscut saw can be operated by one person, but you can work through a tree much more quickly when two experienced men work together. Ecclesiastes 4:9 says, "*Two are better than one because they have a good return for their labor.*"

Is it appropriate for a pastor writing a devotional to quote Joan Baez? She sang, "No man is an island / No man stands alone / Each man's joy is joy to me / Each man's grief is my own / We need one another." It seems so strange that a protest/social justice songwriter could make the truth of our need for each other so evident and poetic, while some Christians will not consider help from others. I hear from small children all the time, "I can do it myself." That is fine when it's a child learning to tie his shoes, but when you're a single mom raising that child, then you should not have to do it alone. There is an African proverb that says, "It takes a village to raise a child." However, the community mentality does not only extend to raising children. Young married couples need support. Parents of teenagers need support. Grown children whose parents are facing challenging years need support. Widows and widowers need assistance. People need a hand-up sometimes. Patients facing health crises need comfort; a family of the sick and dying need compassionate human contact. Nursing care and retirement home residents need someone to listen. It takes a village to…be a village! This brings us back to Galatians 6:12, "*Bear one another's burdens, and thereby fulfill the law of Christ.*" You don't have to write a check to bear a burden. Sometimes all a person needs is your presence. Often at a funeral home or hospice room, a family member does not need to hear our words as much as they need to feel our presence. After the wilderness temptations of Jesus, it says that angels came and ministered to Jesus. We don't know if they said a word to Him or what they did, except they "ministered." Therein lies a lofty goal! Angels are referred to as "ministering spirits." What a great job description!

— ✤ —

My Story

Day 8

Trusting God...
with the Results

After you have suffered for a little while,
the God of all grace, who called you to His
eternal glory in Christ, will Himself perfect,
confirm, strengthen and establish you.

—2 Peter 1:10

I DID NOT TALK MUCH ABOUT the dreaded *C* word. You mention words like *mass* or *tumor*, and most laymen automatically fear the worst. I was already praying for friends and church members who had cancer. My neighbor across the street and sweet church member was bravely fighting the battle. Another of our most precious church members and friend, only months younger than I, was fighting pancreatic cancer. My wife is a breast cancer survivor. She had surgery, treatments, and has been clear for almost seven years, but I still hold my breath and pray about every doctor's visit. Her mother died of cancer. Her grandmother died of cancer. My daddy died of cancer. My aunt died of cancer. We all know people so dear to us that have been destroyed physically by cancer. To hear Dr. Lovell express the reality that we would not be sure until pathology reports were completed after the surgery was still sobering. However, he was very confident that this tumor was most undoubtedly benign. His confidence and words gave me comfort.

Our story: living by grace

There are experiences in life, especially with a medical diagnosis, that we hope for the best, but we can't help but prepare for the worst. Our culture makes it easy to be afraid, even to the level of becoming a hypochondriac. My brother-in-law's mom expressed her morbid concern about "catching prostate cancer." With all the medical dramas on TV and the medical information on the aforementioned internet, it's easy to become discouraged. And then the problem is compounded when some of the most vulnerable also turn on the TV and hear a charlatan preacher who shines his pearly whites into the camera and makes the claim that with enough faith and his blessing, people can escape sickness and poverty and difficulty. And it just so happens that the expression of that faith is proven by sending money to support his TV ministry. My word! Do we expect these people to fly commercial airlines? They talk about the Lord; but they never speak of sin, repentance, submission, and sometimes perseverance and even persecution.

Paul seems to have a conflicting view with the prosperity gospel. In 2 Corinthians 12:10, he says, "*Therefore I take pleasure in infirmities, in reproaches, in necessities, in persecutions, in distresses for Christ's sake: for when I am weak, then am I strong.*" As a matter of fact, the assurance of faithfulness is also the voice that prepares us to expect trouble. Second Timothy 3:12 says, "*Yea, and all that will live godly in Christ Jesus shall suffer persecution.*" If I understand Paul's admonition to young Timothy correctly, then if I never run into trouble because of my conviction and desire to live godly, my report card may not reflect good grades for my life. It does not mean that if you're rude or obnoxious and people give you a hard time in response, that such response qualifies you as a martyr. That probably means you've been a jerk. The qualifier lies within the statement "live godly in Christ Jesus." In other words, if you never have a run-in with the devil, then it may mean you are both going in the same direction. That is how Paul can say he took pleasure in difficulties, and elsewhere he says to have joy during problems. It is why he and Silas could rejoice and sing after being roughed up and in a prison cell in Philippi. Our response to difficulty may be the best witness to the world that is watching us. I doubt the Philippian jailer would have ever come to hear Paul preach, but he saw something different about these men in persecution that caused him to ask, "how can I be saved?"

Sickness can't own me because I belong to Jesus, now and in eternity! I do not look forward to death, but I sure don't dread the results of death. Faith does involve the promise of heaven, but abiding in Christ, living godly during persecution is not about heaven; it's about living faithfully here and now. We'll join ten thousand times ten thousand and thousands of thousands of voices when we praise Jesus in heaven. But what about standing in faith in this life? Sometimes that may mean speaking the truth when your voice is all alone. Second Peter 1 says:

> *Now for this very reason also, applying all diligence, in your faith supply moral excellence, and in your moral excellence, knowledge, and in your knowledge, self-control, and in your self-control, perseverance, and in your perseverance, godliness, and in your godliness, brotherly kindness, and in your brotherly kindness, love. For if these qualities are yours and are increasing, they render you neither useless nor unfruitful in the true knowledge of our Lord Jesus Christ.*

Oh, I do not want to be found useless, nor unfruitful in God's evaluation. So 2 Peter 1:10 is comforting, *"After you have suffered for a little while, the God of all grace, who called you to His eternal glory in Christ, will Himself perfect, confirm, strengthen and establish you."* I can trust Him with the results!

—— ❦ ——

My Story

Day 9

Trusting God...
with the Timing

The greatest among you will be your servant.
For whoever exalts himself will be humbled,
and whoever humbles himself will be exalted.

—Matthew 23:11–12

A FEW DAYS FOLLOWING MY INITIAL visit to Dr. Lovell with Semmes Murphey, October 12, 2019, was the date set to travel to Memphis to have the surgery. It was a few weeks away, which initially gave me pause, but the sweet voice of Ms. Marilyn, Dr. Lovell's nurse, shared that Dr. Lovell did not have an open date for months away. However, he was making arrangements to put a team together to perform my surgery on a Saturday. I know Saturdays are special days for most pastors. Often it may be the only day during the week that we can spend with our family without ministry responsibilities. Often the needs of others demand even Saturday must be yielded. It requires an understanding family and devoted wife to appreciate the priority of ministry. There is no real "day off," and there is never a time when we are not "on call." Through the years, ten different occasions have meant that either I postpone leaving with my family on a planned vacation or left my family to return home early to preach a funeral. I am sure the same sense of sacrifice is true for doctors and their families too. Therefore, the scheduling of a Saturday for my surgery was in itself appreciated.

Our story: living by grace

In America, our founding documents state that our national conscience holds to the truth that we are built upon some common beliefs and convictions. We are all created equal, and every person has God-given rights. We fight to defend each other's rights. It almost feels un-American to expect someone to give up his rights. But we are not called as Christians to put ourselves first. Philippians 2:3–4 holds core-shaking truth for a believer that requires us to think differently than this world. *"Do nothing out of selfish ambition or vain conceit, but in humility consider others better than yourselves. Each of you should look not only to your own interests, but also to the interests of others."* It is this thinking that Romans 12:2 identifies as *"transformed by the renewing of your mind."* The world is saying, "Gimmie, and gimmie more." The selfish life demands to have what I want when I want it because I deserve to get what I want, and I'll hurt whoever I have to in getting what I want! This is the foolish heart, with an attitude that promotes a self-defeating strategy for living whereby people are destroying themselves. This is the attitude of Adam. This is the attitude of our fallen and now natural state. It is the attitude of what Proverbs calls the "fool."

A principle of interpretation for understanding the Bible is to interpret Scripture using Scripture. How do you marry Philippians 2:3–4 to Romans 12:2? The book of James would provide the answer. James 2:18 says, *"You have faith, and I have works; show me your faith without the works, and I will show you my faith by my works."* Displaying faith by works *is* to *"consider others better than yourselves"* and *"renewing of your mind"* happening together. Instead of looking at how to get all you can, why not try to give away what you don't need to somebody who desperately needs your surplus. Make sure the most expensive gift given to your family at Christmas does not actually go to anyone in your family. My family always makes sure the most we spend on a Christmas gift is given to the Lottie Moon Christmas Offering for international missions. When you're preparing a meal at Thanksgiving, fix an extra plate. Carry it to a widow or even better invite her to come to share with your family. At Christmas, contact the BSU, and make the arrangements to invite some international students for a traditional meal at your home. Pick out a single mom in your church with no extended family and invite her and her kids. If you can, host a foreign exchange student for a semester or a year; open your door and your heart to them. Work in a food pantry for a day. Call the jail and arrange to deliver a meal for inmates and guards. When you are paying for your food in the fast-food line, pay for the people in the car behind you. Visit a home-bound person in your church. Visit someone in the nursing home. There are thousands of other little acts of kindness that help change an attitude and practice the ideas that come to a renewed mind.

The secret to considering others by a renewing of your mind in faith and works is to make certain *why* you do what you do "unto the Lord." You renew your mind in the word of God. If you are not giving the best part of your day to a quiet time with God in prayer, some sincere time reading His Word, then you'll never develop a renewed mind, nor the resulting renewed expectation about daily living. If your heart is not changed, your mind will not be renewed, your actions become measured, your joy will not be complete, and we just can't help that our motives become about us, not His glory.

—— ❦ ——

My Story
Day 10

Trusting God...
Patience as a Patient

And the Lord direct your hearts into the love of
God, and into the patient waiting for Christ.

—2 Thessalonians 3:5

THE DAY FINALLY ARRIVED. OUR DAUGHTER and son-in-law, Emily
and Chris, traveled from Shreveport to be with LeeAnn during
the surgery. Our other children, Joshua and Abby, had responsibilities with work. We assured them their mother would keep them
informed. We arrived at the Methodist Hospital in downtown
Memphis early. We parked in what was a deserted garage and walked
into the entrance for the patient check-in. I checked in at a desk that
led to what seemed to be an abandoned waiting room. It was only
minutes before my wife and I were escorted back into the surgical
holding area. I remember thinking, *I hate that these folks probably
gave up a Saturday for my surgery, but from the patient's perspective,
Saturday rules!* The nurse handed me the infamous hospital gown.

The hospital gown must be an accepted secret praxis that medical professionals all over the world have agreed upon as some insider
joke to play on all patients. I've kiddingly referred to these as the
garment that gives the term ICU a whole different meaning. Before

I disrobed to wear this awkward garment, the nurse looked at me and told me to wait. She brought back a different-colored gown. I'm sure she exchanged the gown, not because of the color but because of the size. The hospital probably had either a one-size-fits-most, and she knew I was not a "most," or they have gowns in small, medium, large, extra-large, and then my size labeled simply as "drop cloth." I am not a stranger to adapting to this common hospital problem. When our youngest daughter was born, my wife went into labor so quickly that the nurse who was assigned to get Daddy prepared tied the left and right arms of two gowns together and made a single gown that still barely fit. So on the day of surgery, with my new robe on, I lay on the bed. Beds in the surgical holding area only come in one size. I then waited for what I had secretly dreaded the most: the IV. I know as you read this, you probably have labeled or judged me in some way for my dreading "the needle." But you don't have enough information to make such an assessment. If it were one stick, that quick, then I'd be slick! But I am told I have unusually deep and extremely tough veins. I have survived multiple attempts by multiple nurses who failed to get a needle into me in past experiences. So…I knew this would be a complicated matter. The more you tell hospital staff about past experiences, the more likely you are to get "the look." They don't even know they are giving "the look." Therefore, I try to say it once to the first person in warning, and then just grin and bear it. Hey, at least it's not an MRI. And I know I would certainly look like a sissy if I asked them to wait until I'm asleep to try. I don't think they can do that, but do not believe for a minute that I've not considered asking. Just before the game of hide-and-seek between my veins and the needle, Dr. Lovell came in. He met my wife and talked to both of us and then left to prepare himself to perform the surgery. On his heels, the anesthesiologist spoke with us, and then the needle arrived. The kind nurse tried three times on my left arm to no avail, and finally, she moved to my right arm and hit pay dirt. Now remember I am a bona fide member of the macho-redneck-real-men-don't-cry fraternity, so you'd never know I dreaded the needle. However, on the inside, I was kissing the feet of this nurse who "got it" on the fourth try.

Although I told them not to come, I was not overly surprised when dear and kind friends, Glen and Dianne Brown, from our church, made the early morning drive to Memphis to be with us before the surgery and to sit with my wife during the operation. Bro Glen prayed with us. He and I have been partners in prayer for many years over many parts of life. We've always had a kindred spirit. He always blesses me to be part of an honest, heartfelt, genuine friendship, always undergirded with the third person that meets with us—the Holy Spirit. Glen's prayer is calm and calming. Not long after, I was rolled away to surgery. The next thing I knew, I was in la-la land.

Our story: living by grace

There are some classic illustrations of people in the Bible that had physical needs that were healed by God. The question of debate in our day is, does God still heal miraculously? The ultimate healing will be when God gives us a new resurrection body, and the "former things pass away and all things are made new." The "former things" of sickness, sorrow, death and, most of all, sin will no longer be part of our daily experience. However, in this life, we still live with the effects of the fall of Adam. We're given a new nature, but we also war with the flesh. We still deal with temptation, pride, ego, and sickness. Each experience is an occasion for us to walk by faith and trust God's ever-present power in us to overcome. God never tempts us to do wrong. James 1:14 says, "*Let no man say when he is tempted, I am tempted of God: for God cannot be tempted with evil, neither tempteth he any man.*" God always provides a way out of making the wrong choices. First Corinthians 10:13 says, "*There hath no temptation taken you but such as is common to man: but God is faithful, who will not suffer you to be tempted above that ye are able; but will with the temptation also make a way to escape, that ye may be able to bear it.*" However, there are some occasions when God may test us, not to see if we will do evil but to build our character.

The Bible uses the analogy of a goldsmith or a silversmith. His job is to refine the precious metals and increase their value and guarantee their purity. The goldsmith would place the gold into a vessel and apply extreme heat. As the metal melts under the pressure of the fire, anything that is not gold is separated and rises to the top. The goldsmith skims off the dross as debris and impurities. Eventually, the goldsmith can look into the gold and see no dross, but only the perfect reflection of himself. God is much more concerned with our character than our comfort. Paul is an example of how the modern Christian can understand sickness and physical difficulties. Paul suffered some physical condition, which he asked God to remove. He asked three different occasions for God to remove it. Satan used this affliction to try to "buffet" or tear Paul down. God used it to build Paul's faith. Second Corinthians 12:9 says, *"And he said unto me, My grace is sufficient for thee: for my strength is made perfect in weakness. Most gladly, therefore, will I rather glory in my infirmities, that the power of Christ may rest upon me."* The question we are considering is, does God still heal miraculously? I would submit that *all* healing is temporary, but *all* healing is from God. Jesus healed people out of compassion but also to deliver a more profound message of the Gospel. No matter if God provides healing at the hands of a surgeon or pharmacist, all healing is held in the hand of God. But God uses the thorn in the flesh sometimes to accomplish His higher purpose of bringing glory to His name through our testimony of faith in His grace. It is a great testimony when the world witnesses the inexplicable nobility of a saint living and dying with peace in full confidence of the sufficiency of grace. Death with no sting!

—— ⚜ ——

My Story

Day 11

Trusting God...When Things Go Right

The Lord bless you, and keep you; The
Lord make His face shine on you, and
be gracious to you; The Lord lift up His
countenance on you, and give you peace.

—Numbers 6:24–26

The surgery could not have gone better. Dr. Lovell had prepared my family and me beforehand as to the time needed to operate. He noted that it all depended upon what he found when he performed the laminectomy and then cut through the dura and laid eyes on the tumor as to how long and complicated would be the surgery. He reported to my wife afterward that it could not have gone better. It was a little more than three hours, and I would be in recovery for about an hour before they would move me to an ICU step-down room. I remember waking up and being transported into what I thought was a three-sided room. I remember thinking, *Don't say that out loud*. However, in time, I would learn that was not an anesthesia-induced hallucination. It was pretty much the shape of the room. Another discovery was that I had an active IV in my right arm. I assume it was necessary to have another IV in my left arm, which had been rebellious before the surgery. Apparently, it was still unruly after I was asleep because I discovered in the knuckle of my forefinger on my left hand there was a Hep-Lock. It had no IV hooked up but was wrapped and taped to be used to push meds through the apparatus. For the next forty-eight hours, I had to lay flat on my back. The purpose was to allow the dura, the paper-thin lining around my spinal cord time to seal.

I remember being grateful for a Foley catheter, as odd as that sounds. I drank water through a straw, and they tell me I drank a lot of water. To ward off evil spirits (kidney stones) I drink one and a half gallons of water every day of my life anyway. Today I drank more. Hey, if you have a Foley, use it! Oh, the water was so good! LeeAnn tried to feed me, but do you know how hard it is to eat flat on your back? I hope it was actual food LeeAnn was dropping in my mouth. I'm sure I looked like a baby bird eating a worm; okay, maybe a baby Big Bird, but it was difficult all the same. I had to hold my water cup next to my left ear to drink while remaining flat. More than once, I put the straw in my mouth, and no matter how hard I pulled on that straw, I couldn't get any water. I pulled the cup back and inspected it. It looked fine, so I tried again. Then I realized I didn't have the straw in my mouth. I had the Hep-Lock from my knuckle in my mouth! Thankfully, I did not draw out any blood.

I remember bits and pieces of the next hours and days that seem now more like a dream. My wife told me others had been there from our church. Her sister's family—Amy, Alan, and Lynn—came and sat with me while my family ate a meal. It all seems like a vague alternate reality, which I'm sure was a result of pain medicine because they were pumping me full of something different every hour and on the hour. Now I'm a talker, but I'm told I become extremely chatty when I'm on drugs. I've never used drugs outside of those medically prescribed. I will hardly take those when I get home after any surgery or procedure in the past. My dad became medically dependent upon phenobarbital. It was all they had back in 1964. Better drugs were developed, but he had an addiction to phenobarbital by then. He could not help that, but it did play into our reality. But my dad also struggled with alcoholism for a time in his life. It almost tore our family apart. Prescription drugs and liquor and bipolarity make for a roller-coaster life in a family, thus my hesitation with pain medication. I have never let wine, liquor, or beer touch my lips. I cannot quite fathom the concept behind "recreational drugs," except maybe sucking the helium out of a balloon and sounding like a Smurf?

Along with the family history and fear of ever opening the door to becoming dependent, there are some immediate and practical reasons why I don't like painkillers. Painkillers make me sick. I would much prefer hurting than throwing up. I have always had a very high tolerance for pain. However, I also must have a high resistance to pain medication. One rather delicate example happened a few years ago when I was awake during the beginning of a procedure. They gave me Versed combined with Fentanyl, which is commonly known as conscious sedation or twilight sleep. However, I was fully awake and aware of everything going on, and they started the procedure. I finally was prepared to surrender my macho-redneck-real-men-don't-cry fraternity card and say something.

I said, "Should I be feeling this?"

To which, the doctor blurted out, "Give that guy more medicine. He's a big man."

I soon drifted off. For the rest of that particular day, I don't remember getting dressed afterward nor the ride home nor anything else that day. So I guess it came as no surprise, as the Methodist Hospital nurses moved up the chart of pain meds, that they were either impressed or aggravated with my endurance. I'm not sure. I do remember one nurse giving me a fourth shot of morphine and saying "this should do it" and then coming back in a few minutes to say she was calling the doctor. It was almost like I was in trouble now! Finally, they arrived with Dilaudid. I know people grow addicted to pain relievers, so it's nothing to joke about, but Dilaudid became my friend for the next two days.

Our story: living by grace

The Bible prepares us for the spiritual battle that has been raging since Lucifer rebelled; since Adam and Eve ate the fruit of disobedience, and from the first moment, each one of us sided with our sinful nature. The Bible describes putting on the armor of God (Ephesians 6:11–17). Armor is to protect a soldier in battle. The Bible warns about the dangerous enemy, like a lion who wants to devour us (1 Peter 5:8). We should always be prepared to engage in battle. However, there are also occasions when God answers prayer *"immeasurably more than all we ask or imagine"* (Ephesians 3:20). There are occasions when God works a miracle; when God saves us from harm. We should not wait until we go to heaven to realize we are in His presence! We should praise Him every day; thank Him for every moment! I remember every spanking my parents gave me. I deserved them all. However, those disciplinary events, although filled with drama at that moment, are now overshadowed with memories of all the laughter and fun and joyful experiences instead. Do not let the joy of God's goodness and blessing escape the moment without knowing His smile upon your soul. I do not mean to sound irreverent, but consider a question: Do you ever think of God laughing? I know we all have seen some anthropomorphic image of white hair and a bearded image of God sitting in heaven with a lightning bolt ready to strike. Maybe you can imagine God shaking his head, telling us "No!" or displaying being ashamed or angry over all of our great sins and spiritual failures. But do you ever imagine God laughing? If the lightning bolt is the image of an instrument of judgment we all fear, then I will submit that I'm going to imagine the thunder that rattles the windows is God's laughter! Ventriloquist and Impressionist can sound like other people. I always thought Rich Little was funny. But if I could only learn one sound that resembles God's voice, I'd be hard-pressed *not* to choose His laughter! I'm a big boy; I laugh big. I believe God laughs big too!

We live in a world that needs to hear the truth about sin and repentance and judgment and hell and all those realities. We also live in a world that needs to hear about God's love, and forgiveness, and acceptance in Christ…and they need to hear God laugh! The only way some will ever do so, is to witness our lives, surrendered and living godly, in righteousness, wholesome, pure, genuine, the real-deal Christian walk. The world needs to see a life that loves to talk about blessings; the person that loves to be an encourager; a friend that compliments and wants to meet the needs of others with joy. But the world needs to hear that a Christian can laugh because we have a God who laughs and enjoys and loves and blesses, and He loves us! And "God so loved the world," too.

If you have any trouble believing Jesus laughed, then picture in your mind's eye (if you can ever get the speck or the beam out); imagine the scene from Luke 18 of the little children coming to Jesus.

> *People brought babies to Jesus, hoping he might touch them. When the disciples saw it, they shooed them off. Jesus called them back. Let these children alone. Don't get between them and me. These children are the kingdom's pride and joy. Mark this: Unless you accept God's kingdom in the simplicity of a child, you'll never get in. (Luke 18:16 The Message)*

— ⚜ —

My Story
Day 12

Trusting God...When Your Heart Breaks

Who shall separate us from the love of Christ?

—Romans 8:35

AFTER MY FORTY-EIGHT HOURS OF BEING flat on my back, I was so looking forward to being able to move and then sit up and then stand up and then walk. I had a crucial twofold reason which motivated me to work through these parameters in rapid form. First, my sanity! Have you ever laid flat for forty-eight hours? I wanted to move. And second, I was avoiding the hospital bedpan, at all costs. A nurse came to start me on that journey to mobility by first removing my friend, the Foley catheter. However, she did not prepare me for what was to come. I did not realize they had the tube not only draining the contents of my bladder but also somehow had it connected to my toes. I'm sure of it because she pulled about five feet of tubing out. She told me to take a deep breath and then let it out. I'm sure when I exhaled, ships in the nearby Mississippi River wondered why a fog horn was blowing. At that moment, I could not decide if she was Nurse Ratched from *One Flew Over the Cuckoo's Nest* or Annie Wilkes from Stephen King's *Misery*. Nevertheless, with the unexpected deed executed, my path was set in motion. Within thirty minutes, I had completed all the steps to fulfill my quest. As I got back into bed in my triangle-shaped room, my wife's phone rang. Her phone had been ringing for the past two days. We are a blessed family and have a great extended family, and I've been a pastor for thirty-seven years, so we have some great friends all over Mississippi. This call turned out not to be a welcomed message. It was from my sister Donna to deliver the sad news that our oldest sister, Judy, had died. My heart was broken!

Our story: living by grace

The doctrine, which is known as the total depravity of man, is a hotly debated topic among theologians. The way I understand the basis of it is not surrounding the question, "Is there any good found in men's deeds?" It simply means to me that there is nothing about me that has not been touched by the fall of man or by sin. I may do the most gracious and kind act toward another person, but if I pridefully share the glory for doing the deed, then I've robbed God of the glory. The Sermon on the Mount makes it clear that you do not have to bring an act to fruition to make it a sin. "If you have anger in your heart," then you don't have to commit murder physically to cross the line. In that perspective on sin, then we are left without hope outside of the redemptive work of grace. If spiritual death is the manifestation of separation from God, then outside of the restoration Christ gives in faith by His death, burial, and resurrection, as Paul says in 1 Corinthians 15:17–19, "*And if Christ be not raised, your faith is vain; ye are yet in your sins. Then they also which are fallen asleep in Christ are perished. If in this life only we have hope in Christ, we are of all men most miserable.*" But praise God there is *hope* found in Christ. It is hope resulting in the truth that we are of all men most *joyful*. Christ is raised, and He lives in *me*, and I abide in *Him*. My life is changed because of my relationship with Christ. But thank God everything beyond this life is also changed. I will never be separated from the love of God (Romans 8:35–39). He will never leave me nor forsake me (Hebrews 13:5). He has a home eternal prepared in His presence for those who trust Him (John 14).

It is not a question *of* grief coming into our lives. Job 14:1 says, *"Man that is born of a woman is of few days and full of trouble."* The question is what to do when we stand at the brink of sorrow? Will we allow our feelings to lie to us to say there is no hope? Like Gideon, we all may feel abandoned in times of trouble, *"Oh my Lord, if the Lord be with us, why then is all this befallen us? and where be all his miracles which our fathers told us of"* (Judges 16:13). These moments are a test for us. Will we give authority to our feelings or our faith?

Who is leading us? Psalm 23 is the familiar passage read at gravesides around the world. There is hope found in the famous statement of verse 4, *"Yea, though I walk through the valley of the shadow of death, I will fear no evil: for thou art with me; thy rod and thy staff they comfort me."* What a wonderful promise; we arrive at the darkest place—*"the valley of the shadow"*—we will not be there alone. We fear no evil; we don't have to be afraid. Our Shepherd will be there with us. He will provide our comfort. *But* to find the promises and hope found in verse 4, don't miss how one arrives at the place of hope. Psalm 23:3 comes first, *"He leadeth me in the paths of righteousness for his name's sake."* We don't have to face death alone. But praise God, *He leads*! We don't have to face life alone either!

—— ⚜ ——

My Story
Day 13

Trusting God...in Sorrow with Family

Take My yoke upon you, and learn from
Me, for I am gentle and humble in heart;
and you shall find rest for your souls.

—Matthew 11:29

As I write about the experience of my sister's death, it is still a little raw for me emotionally. Judy and I shared a birthday, which at the time of her death was coming up in a few weeks. I had always told her that I must have been the best birthday present she ever received. She didn't always agree with me on that statement and would one-up me with the rebuttal that she had changed my diapers. I never quite understood the glory in her claim. Judy was fourteen years older than me. I doubt she changed many of my diapers, but there was no doubt that we came from the same stock, and we loved each other deeply. I was hurting for Donna. I was hurting for Andy and Daniel, Judy's sons. LeeAnn and I spent a great deal of time with Andy and Daniel when they were young. Judy was going to school to become a nurse, which she started a little later in life than most. Jim was a manager in the restaurant business. I guess after selling insurance for many years, the stress of the pizza business was a piece of cake, or I guess better, a slice of pie. I could not stand the thought of my family standing alone at my sister's funeral.

I shared with the medical staff that I needed to leave the hospital, but they refused until I could walk the distance around the hallway. So immediately I struck out on the excursion. It was my first trip out of my room. I held my IV pole, and LeeAnn held the back of my "ICU robe" so as not to scare anyone in the hallway. I walked the full circumference of the pentagon-shaped hall on the ninth floor. If they would not have shaped the rooms like triangles, then it would have been a straighter path, but it would not have mattered. At that moment, if they told me I had to walk a mile, I was determined. The fact of pushing myself may explain why this is not the end of my story. After my journey, the hospital staff began making the arrangements for my discharge. After arriving at home, I preached Judy's funeral. I honestly do not remember much about the experience. Some bits and pieces have the fabric of a dream, with the pain of reality attached. But I'm thankful for that precious time with my family.

Our story: living by grace

In my lifetime, the idea of the all-American family has changed. I grew up watching *Leave it to Beaver*. All right, the only true-to-life character was Eddie Haskell, the sneaky, two-faced kid who was always stirring up trouble. If you did not know that character among your peers growing up, it means you *were* that kid. Television seldom shows the real story, but we escape to its mind-numbing trappings anyway. In the '80s, there was such hope about the positive influence of *The Cosby Show*. Now we've learned the reality of the monster behind that show. For many families, that's what growing up is really like; we put on a show for the rest of the world, but we hide the monsters of reality, sometimes from ourselves.

The only hope for any family to reach their fullest potential is found in Christ, by faith and following. Please do not misunderstand what I'm saying. There are lost people who love each other and who love their families. *And* some people are Christians but do not follow God's plan for the family, but they still survive. *And* none of us follow perfectly the plan of God. *But* when we do, we find something this world can never supply. My family is the same way. I wish I could say I have been the perfect son, brother, husband, and father, but I have too many living family members to call me out on that lie. However, by God's grace, we have the potential and the grace to love each other with such deep affection that we can work through anything. First Peter 4:8 says, "*And above all things have fervent love among yourselves: for love shall cover the multitude of sins.*" During the good times of the busyness of life, it is so easy to allow the busyness to crowd out the essential spiritual mooring of life. During the difficult times of life, without that foundation, families turn to the disposable climate of our culture.

We fill the landfills because we don't mind throwing away anything, even marriages, children, and families. Everyone is part of a family. If you are single and your family is in heaven, then you should still be a part of a family—your church family. Anyone of us can find an excuse to throw away our relationships in our sinful selfishness. It is hard work to live out our commitments. But when we do, the rewards of peace and joy and love and fulfillment make life so precious. And when death does come for our loved ones, then there is no regret, only anticipation of a blessed reunion.

—— ✣ ——

My Story

Day 14

Trusting God...in Sorrow with Friends

And the ransomed of the Lord will return
and come with joyful shouting to Zion,
with everlasting joy upon their heads.
They will find gladness and joy, And
sorrow and sighing will flee away.

—Isaiah 35:10

FAST FORWARD ALMOST FIVE WEEKS INTO my recovery. I had returned three weeks earlier to Oxford to have staples removed and received the thumbs-up from Dr. Lovell to return to activity with which I was comfortable. I had completed four sessions of physical therapy and had pushed myself a little harder each day. I had been back in the pulpit for two weeks. I was moving slowly but had visited hospitals and nursing homes and even back in my office for part of the day for about two weeks. I was undoubtedly on the road to recovery.

Our dear friend Donna Harris, who had bravely battled pancreatic cancer, was called home to heaven. I was so sad, as was our entire community. I had visited with her husband and family, whom I hold dear to my heart as their pastor. I preached her funeral to a congregation as packed into our sanctuary as I've ever seen. There were probably six hundred plus seeking comfort. I attempted to direct them to remember the joy Donna had brought to each of us while pointing them to the truth of the Gospel message and the Lord where and in whom Donna found her joy. However, I returned home that evening sad myself. I have been the pastor of First Baptist Church in West Point, Mississippi, for over sixteen years. West Point is our home. I moved from my childhood home at the age of seventeen to attend college and never moved back. It will not be much longer that I will have lived in West Point longer than anywhere in my lifetime.

People probably do not think about how death and funerals affect the pastor. We smile and seek to proclaim the truth and hope beyond this life in Christ. However, the same God who gave every church member an emotional being in their soul made pastors in the same way. It's hard to comfort someone when your head is hanging low, so the Lord gifts most pastors with a delayed response in our emotions. But everyone has to allow for a healthy outlet for grief and sorrow to be released. I had not yet had a good grieving cry over my own sister Judy. I am an ugly crier, so usually I do that alone.

Our story: living by grace

Some people live in the same town all of their lives. That is not usually true for people called to ministry. Some pastors have never lived anywhere longer than three or four years. However, I've believed that there are significant advantages to long-term commitments and long tenures. I served Grace Memorial Baptist Church in Gulfport, Mississippi, for ten years before the Lord called us to West Point. West Point has been our home for over sixteen years. I am now the longest-tenured pastor in the history of FBC. It is funny how churches have many of the same people but with different faces and names. There are always people who are wise and measured and dependable. There's always the good-natured man or woman who loves to joke and "pick" at people but loves to have people reciprocate and "pick" back. You have a handful of folks who are negative about everything. You have a bucketful of folks who are positive about everything. Some folks are the Marthas of the church—very practical and get things done. You'll find them organizing and rallying people to serve. Then you have the Marys of the church. These are the people who are meek, calm, and it becomes apparent they are accustomed to sitting at the feet of Jesus. But in fifty-nine years of being in church, thirty-seven as a pastor, four years as a minister of youth and music, I have never encountered anyone quite like Donna Harris. Of all the people I can think of in our church, there will be no one missed like Donna.

Donna was a talker, unlike anybody I've ever known. But she was genuine, and if you didn't like her, she didn't care; she was going to like you and talk to you anyway. She loved her family so deeply. She loved West Point. She loved her church. She loved her friends. She loved her Lord. She was a true friend.

We all have those exceptional, unique people in our lives that when they die, especially when that person dies at a young age, then all kinds of emotions are triggered. You ask questions that do not have satisfying answers. You question God about fairness. Why is this person taken and a drunk pedophile lives to old age? When you start down that path, it does not lead to a good place. During those times, we wear blinders to focus on pain at the moment. However, to find peace, we must also allow the truth to be acknowledged. I'm not implying that we should crowd out the feelings of sorrow and sadness or even unreasonable questions with a quick response of truth. Sorrow and grief are part of our emotional makeup. But while we ask all those questions, even some that are a little unhealthy, we must allow truth to sit in the same room. We must wait, knowing in the back of our mind that truth is present…until the right time when *we are ready to hear truth in our soul* as well as our mind.

The truth is we are all sinners (Romans 3:23), and the payment of sin is death (Romans 6:23). So if we *only* allow the question of fairness, then we will never find peace. We have to allow the entire truth of Romans 6:23 as a whole to set in: "*But the gift of God is eternal life through Jesus Christ our Lord.*" Sin brought sickness and death. Jesus brought life. Grief and sorrow focus inwardly on how this situation makes me feel and what I'm missing and will miss and what I want, and it's *not this*! Those are legitimate feelings and true to our natural self. But...that natural self no longer governs us. We are born again. We are new creatures. We are believers. We are the family of God; we are the children of God. We are called to rise above those feelings by faith and allow faith to have authority over our feelings. We are called to allow truth to speak in love and address what we *know* over what we *feel*. And what we *know* is that this life is temporary. We will not live in this state of being forever. This life is a dress rehearsal for eternity. What we decide here in this life matters significantly about how we will translate into eternal life, but it is selfish to think only in light of today and the here and now. Instead of focusing on what I will miss here on this earth without the person I miss, we must become more minded for eternity. From a heavenly perspective, we can try to imagine all the ways we are going to enjoy the reunion when death will no longer even be a consideration. *Then* we allow that to grow into a conviction that wants to live a better life because of the example our loved one has left for us. We should aspire to be that kind of person to someone else. If you had a godly mother, then aspire to be a godly mother. I had a righteous grandpa. I want my grandchildren to remember me in the same way that I remember him. Well, that doesn't just happen. That kind of influence requires being present in their lives and loving them like I was loved. It requires me to guide them with the example I witnessed, invest in them so they can reap the dividend as I have for my lifetime.

Death is always an enemy, and if we allow it, death will rattle our faith. We can waste our time in anger and bitterness and disappointment. Looking ahead to the reality of our mortality can be a teacher to train us with clarity while we are living. Death can sound an alarm that our days are numbered, and we have to live to the fullest. Donna Harris told me early in the discovery of her cancer that God had control of her life. God had already numbered her days. She believed she had just as many days as God would allow her. She decided she was going to live each day to the fullest. And she did! Donna lived up to the frequent admonition of her mother, Mrs. Eva—"Be sweet and act nice." I hope when the time comes to stand at that darkest place for your family, you will know you do not stand there alone. Allow truth to have his proper place to speak to your heart in due time to produce hope, comfort, and renewal to get ready for eternity!

—— ✤ ——

My Story

Day 15

Trusting God...When Things Suddenly Go Wrong

But the salvation of the righteous is from the
Lord; He is their strength in time of trouble.

—Psalm 37:39

THE DATE WAS NOVEMBER 9, 2019. It was a Saturday night, and I
was lying on my bed watching LSU beat Alabama in football. I am a
Mississippi State fan, but we've not had a banner year, even by MSU
standards. My loyalty is not so deep to MSU that I hate any other
team. I cheer for MSU first, but then I cheer for Ole Miss outside of
the Egg Bowl, and then SEC Western Conference teams, then SEC
teams against whomever. I enjoy watching college sports, but I do
not lose sleep over a win or a loss. That night I was lying flat on my
back on my bed, and I coughed. It was not even a particularly deep
cough. However, when I coughed, I felt as if that Tasmanian devil
had returned and thrust a knife through my incision in my back. It
was enough to make me stand up. People look for defining moments
in life. That cough was a defining moment for me.

It has become a family trait that when a Funderburg does something, we go full-bore. We go the whole hog; we go big or go home. We
laugh big. We talk loudly. We cry ugly. When we throw up, our neigh-

59

bors know what's happening. My mama often chided me for blowing my nose too hard, for sneezing so dramatically, and for coughing so deeply. She often said, "You're going to hurt yourself doing that." Well…Mama was right. The discovery of the tumor started with a sneeze. Now the next chapter of my saga began with a cough.

Our story: living by grace

We sometimes are tempted to think life is not fair because the standard by which we measure fairness is not fair! When I tell someone that I'm five feet seventeen inches, it is confusing because it messes with how they think of measurements. We should be glad God does not use our standards for righteousness or fairness. Isaiah 55:9 says, *"For as the heavens are higher than the earth, so are my ways higher than your ways, and my thoughts than your thoughts."* In 1970, Lynn Anderson sang, "I beg your pardon / I never promised you a rose garden." The country song crossed over to be an international hit. The lyrics go on to say, "Along with the sunshine / there's got to be a little rain sometimes." Well, Adam and Eve were in a garden, and the roses did not have thorns. It was perfect. They were perfect. That is why the first time Adam saw Eve, he said, "Wooo! Man!" God gave them the freedom to enjoy everything in that garden with only one exception: the tree of knowledge of good and evil. You know the story of Genesis 3. The tree was a test. The devil manipulated the test and made it a temptation with his lies and twisting of God's word. Adam and Eve failed, and something within them died at that moment. They became mortal and sinners. Maybe the final words of Genesis 2 best capture the perfection before they sinned, "They were not ashamed." After they sinned, everything changed. Responses they would have never considered before were their first reaction, words like "cover-up" and "hid themselves" and "afraid." New thoughts filled their minds, like blame: "The woman…that You gave me." And Eve coined the phrase long before Flip Wilson, "The devil made me do it." There were new consequences, like pain in childbirth and work that has now become filled with thorns and thistles, a burden of toil. And the most devastating impact, a changed relationship with

God, a change that was a direct result of the fallen state that Adam had chosen, and the catastrophic consequence of spiritual separation and also physical death. In all fairness, God should have left man in the state which Adam had chosen. That would have been *fair*! But God did not. An act of mercy and extension of grace is heard in the final words of Genesis 3. God protects man from eating from the tree of life. Driving them from the garden was to keep them from being sustained forever in their pitiful state of the curse of sin. God was not acting out of fairness. He was working out of merciful grace!

When difficulties come (hard times of working ninety hours a week without successful results and no appreciation for the hard work); when sickness brings pain and suffering; when it seems like you can't catch a break; when relationships fall apart, and the world falls out from under your feet; when it looks like your prayers cannot get past your ceiling, and you cry out to God and finally say, "It's just not fair," hear Romans 5:8, "*But God demonstrated his love toward us, in that, while we were yet sinners, Christ died for us.*" Adam chose to disobey by his lack of action to protect Eve and then by going along and eating the fruit he was given. He knew the consequences, and he did it anyway. Whatever you are feeling is *not fair* is the result of that choice. But God's thoughts and ways are better—even "*while we were yet sinners.*" God provides redemption in the finished work of Christ. *In* Christ, you find better than fairness; you find forgiveness and abundance (John 10:10).

My Story
Day 16

Trusting God...
in Physical Pain

Father, if thou be willing, remove
this cup from me: nevertheless not
my will, but thine, be done.

—Luke 22:42

MY AUNT CELIA FAE WOULD OFTEN say, "Oh, I've got a tickle in my throat." Then she would eat a bite of something not recommended for a person with diabetes or a heart patient to eat. It was usually a fried chicken liver or a bite of cake. My cough was not much more than a natural response to a tickle in my throat. I went to bed that Saturday night earlier than my usual early bedtime because, as we say in the south, I felt a headache "coming on." I guess technically if one feels a problem "coming on," it is already a headache, but we know it's going to get worse. I took some Tylenol, which I seldom do, and I went to bed. When I lay down, in a few minutes, the headache was better, and I went to sleep.

On Sunday mornings, I do not have a choice to stay home because of a headache. I am the pastor, and besides, I felt I had been on the sideline with this spinal tumor too much as it was. So I took more Tylenol and went to church and enjoyed myself. God always gives grace to endure whatever lies before me. He showed up and showed out that Sunday. Most people don't realize the pastor is the most surprised person in the building when God chooses to use us. We had an excellent worship service. When I got home, I went to bed with the belief that an ordained nap was the most spiritual thing I could do at that time. When I lay down, my headache got better. Sunday evening, we had a special event with the youth drama team and children's activity to pack Operation Christmas Child boxes together. LeeAnn and I stayed for the first part but left early. By the next morning, I could hardly stand for more than a few minutes before the headache returned, and it was becoming unbearable. I called Semmes Murphey Clinic and left a message for Dr. Lovell. His nurse responded and told me it sounded like I had a CSF leak.

Now the medical profession uses so many acronyms and initials that one might think they are speaking in code just to make the rest of us feel inferior. If my head had not hurt so, I would have asked if a CSF leak would leave a stain in my carport. It sounded more like an automobile issue than medical. However, she explained it is a cerebrospinal fluid leak. It is when the dura, the lining around the spinal cord, has a tear, and spinal fluid is leaking out. As the spinal fluid leaks downward, the brain has less fluid to cushion it, and the brain drops, thus the spinal headache. I knew I heard a thud after I coughed. It was my brain dropping. All right, mine was more of a tink than a thud. She explained that a CSF leak often resolves spontaneously if the patient lies flat, which would neutralize the pressure, so the headache is better and gives time for the dura to seal itself. This solution made sense, so I tried it for four days. By Friday morning, I was no better. Dr. Lovell's nurse called. She explained the only reasonable solution would require me to return to Memphis and have a drain inserted to facilitate dealing with the spinal fluid leak and would also require another surgery to repair the damaged dura. I agreed because I was becoming desperate.

After hanging up the phone, I closed my Barlow pocket knife and placed the Gorilla glue back on the shelf...because I was considering an attempt at a home remedy. I called LeeAnn at work, and as soon as she came home, we loaded up a few items and headed back to Methodist Hospital in Memphis. Most married men will understand what I mean when I say "a few items." I had all I needed in a backpack, including a laptop, iPad, a Bible, my CPAP machine, and some extra drawers and PJs. After LeeAnn put her "few things" in the van, we looked like *The Beverly Hillbillies'* vehicle riding down Rodeo Drive after striking black gold. All we needed was Granny sitting in the rocking chair on top.

Our story: living by grace

I hope you will forgive the length of this devotional thought. This subject of pain and our response is something I feel very passionate about, but for me to speak the words that follow during a worship service just feels self-serving. This work is the first medium by which I have expressed the thoughts that follow. So please do not misunderstand—I am not holding myself up as a standard to follow regarding this subject. As Paul said, only follow me when and because I'm following Jesus.

After a plane crash or a train wreck, investigators go to great lengths to identify the cause of the calamity. The black box contains the data that can help them understand the situation. Recordings of the pilots in those minutes before the tragedy are telling. The record of all the instruments helps investigators know the underlying reason for what happened.

There are circumstances in our lives that we want to do the same thing. We know what has happened, but we also want to know *why*. In the broadest sense, we all know what the "black box" is going to reveal. It all traces back to Adam and the consequences of sin. I know that sounds like a broken record, but Adam broke the record—that is the truth. *But*…most of the train wrecks of my life give evidence of *my* culpability by *my* choices, so I can't put it all on Adam. However, there are some experiences in our lives that just happen because we are alive. About these experiences, we know *what* happens, but there's not a right answer to the specific and personal *why* it happened. The devil will use those times to try to tear us down. The Lord will use those experiences to build our faith. God builds character and confidence in *Him.* Our flesh can be self-destructive in self-pity or denial or bitterness or attempts to blame others. Physical pain is one of those experiences that can bring out the worst in us. You may be able to identify the physiological cause, but the intensity of the pain may demand more than a reasonable answer. The most natural response to physical pain is the desire for relief—make the pain go away! Is it wrong to ask to be healed? Is it unfaithful to pray for the pain to go away? Of course not. In Luke 22, in the garden of Gethsemane, Jesus gives us the example of praying faithfully. He asked for the cup he was enduring to be removed—that is very specific and clearly understood as the request for relief. But you cannot miss the qualifiers that reveal the heart of the prayer. He says, *"If it is possible"*—in other words, if this complies with the Father's purpose and plan. If any doubt, Jesus himself prayed, *"Nevertheless, not my will, but thine be done."* I have never experienced pain that I did *not* ask God for relief. My only hope is for the transformation of my heart to reflect the same desire that Christ expressed, "not my will but thine be done."

Pain attacks in specific places, but our entire body will respond. A three-millimeter kidney stone can make a person who is usually a soft-spoken, mild-mannered gentle soul turn into the culmination between an aggressive grizzly bear, a spider, a snake, *Jaws*, and whatever is your most scary movie monster. Mine has to be Bumble, the abominable snow monster from *Rudolf the Red-Nosed Reindeer*, after Hermey the Dentist Elf pulled his teeth. Yikes!

Pain brings out our most selfish mean spirit—the worst in us. It brings out our most natural response. However, for believers, we are not governed by our innate responses. I cannot claim to be an expert in many things, but this is something about which I know. God has given me a very high tolerance for pain. And I have had a lot of experiences to determine that theory to be true. I've had 220 kidney stone episodes to date. My gall bladder ruptured, and a stone became trapped, resulting in pancreatitis, and through the years, I've experienced four other episodes of pancreatitis. I was struck by a car while walking through a parking garage, giving me a grade 3 concussion and breaking my back at L3. I've had a hernia that strangulated and required emergency surgery. I have suffered heart attacks and a

TIA, or min-stroke. I have suffered from migraine headaches and spinal headaches. I've had ingrown toenails, and once I had a splinter in my little finger. There, I think I've covered the gamut. But what I have learned is that pain is no excuse for me to be…well, me. I'm not my own. I don't belong to myself. I am a child of God, born again in Christ. I have the Holy Spirit indwelling me. Galatians 5:22–23 says, *"But the fruit of the Spirit is love, joy, peace, patience, kindness, goodness, faithfulness, gentleness, self-control; against such things, there is no law."* Do some people see "self-control" as a strange inclusion in this list—*self*? Does *self* have a place here? Shouldn't the Holy Spirit control us? That sounds very spiritual, but faith is also practical. You cannot remove the call for your submission to Christ every single day and in every circumstance out of the equation. That is what it means when Jesus calls, *"If any man will come after me, let him deny himself, and take up his cross daily, and follow me"* (Luke 9:23). It is not just when we are in control of the moment but in our worst experience. Self-control is the release valve. We can't help when the intensity of pain makes us subject to temptation, but we can choose to keep our mouths shut! We may not be able to control the pain, but we can control how we choose to respond to others in our suffering. You may ask, "How about when you are on pain medication, and you do not really know what you are saying?" I know my thoughts are going to sound a little legalistic and judgmental, possibly, so allow me to qualify this as what I feel about *my heart*—and mine alone—in my situation. If I do not want anything to proceed out of my mouth when I'm not in control, then I must guard my heart when I am in control. I need to guard my heart and mind every day. I should never allow words that are unbecoming to cross my lips any day or dwell in my heart in any situation. Matthew 15:18 says, *"Those things which proceed out of the mouth come forth from the heart."* I indeed may not be responsible for what I say when I'm on medication, but I am responsible for what I allow to come into my heart. I am responsible for the attitude I take when I am in my proper senses. I can choose how I respond when I hit my thumb with a hammer. I can choose what words I allow into my daily vocabulary. My grandmother had a *word* that she let fly pretty regularly. I would call it more of a barnyard word. I've heard that word as crude as it may be, but it was in context on the farm. However, I've also heard it in response to a host of other occasions. As a kid, I couldn't help myself but giggle when I heard that word from my grandmother. But I said that word once, and I got in all kinds of trouble. I cannot choose to allow little pet sins to hang around in my mind, or my mouth will reveal them. I can choose what words I allow movies and television programs to try to normalize. I can choose what message I will enable the music lyrics to preach to my soul. I can decide if I laugh at the off-color joke a friend tells and allow it to appear as approval. The reason we must guard our eyes and guard our ears is that we are actually guarding our hearts.

Allow me one disclaimer, an exception: some have the terrible and cruel enemy of dementia or Alzheimer's that rob them of memories and steal away the personality of who they are in this world. Sometimes the words they speak are filtered through these terrible diseases. Grace and mercy should be the filters through which we hear these sad moments. Do not judge their heart by their words but through grace. My mama was the kindest woman I have ever known. She was gentle. But dementia became an unwelcome part of her last few years. There were times that old memories of hurt and pain caused by times of indiscretion and unfaithfulness of my daddy resurfaced. My mama had forgiven my daddy. However, the disease manipulated my mama to believe I was not her son, but I was my daddy. Her entire being was transported to a place of deep hurt. The words she probably never even said to my daddy resurfaced, and she said them to me. The things my mother said and did at those moments still embarrass me. I had to go look up a few of the names she called my daddy, vicariously through my ears. And those words came from the same voice that had spoken all the precious words of love and encouragement throughout my lifetime. First Peter 4:8 says, *"Love covers a multitude of sin."* We do not blame a baby who spits upon us. Babies cannot help that. The same attitude is what I tried to adopt when my sweet mama hit those rough spots. Grace is never a wrong response.

— ✻ —

My Story

Day 17

Trusting God... with Frustration

In thee, O Lord, do I put my trust; let me never
be ashamed: deliver me in thy righteousness.

—Psalm 31:1

WHEN WE ARRIVED AT THE METHODIST Hospital in Memphis, there
was some confusion about paperwork and orders. The first time I
entered these doors weeks ago, I thought Saturday morning ruled,
from the patient's perspective. Friday afternoon stinks! The result of
this search for missing orders resulted in our sitting in the admis-
sions area for four hours. I was not a happy camper. The three-hour
trip was difficult, but the waiting room was even less equipped than
LeLe's van. I lay on the floor, praying for relief from the spinal headache or for the miniature Zamboni which they were using to clean
the floors might run me over. Whichever came first would have been
welcomed. The hospital staff was very apologetic and kind. My sweet
wife was probably embarrassed to sit by what looked like a homeless
man at her feet, spread out like a bear in hibernation, but she never
batted an eye.

By the time a room became available, it was shift change. Shift
change in a hospital setting resembles a pee-wee t-ball game between

the inns. One team takes the field, and the other team leaves the field. There is a lot of confusion, but eventually, everyone gets a snack. The night nurses came in fussing at the day nurses because nobody had gotten my vital signs or started an IV or filled out any paperwork. We had only been in the room for a few minutes, but I knew this would be a long night. There was an argument outside my door. I believe it was Redd Fox and Joan Rivers from the language I heard. Soon my door opened, and "Joan" was my nurse. It is going to be an l-o-n-g night. How can I describe her voice? It was a cross between Carol Channing and Fran Drescher. Her voice did something to make my right leg jitter, and my forehead felt like cheese graters were dragging across it. However, as the night progressed, she turned out to be my strong advocate, and I would need one. She was a good nurse.

The orders for the lumbar drain to be inserted were AWOL. The resident doctor who worked with Dr. Lovell came in. She was a very attractive young…very young doctor for what I assumed was at this very advanced point of her training, despite looking so young. The young…very young doctor explained what would happen when she placed the drain in my spine to relieve the pressure, but first, the paperwork had to be found. The young…very young doctor told me once the drain was inserted, I needed to remain flat on my back. The drain mechanism would be placed a bit higher than my horizontal position in the bed. I've referenced that I am six five tall (or five feet seventeen inches on most handwritten paperwork). But I'm still a relatively thick, barrel-chested guy. So my drain was still pretty high on the pole. The young…very young doctor told me if I stood up, the drain would increase in pressure exponentially, and that my brain stem could be sucked through the foramen magnum of the occiput at the base of the skull. In her straightforward words, "that would be a terrible way to leave this world." This young…very young doctor had my attention.

Our story: living by grace

Proverbs 21:5 (NLT) says, "*Good planning and hard work lead to prosperity, but hasty shortcuts lead to poverty.*" In other words, "Plan your work and work your plan." However, another saying is an adaptation from Robert Burns and is a frustrating reality, "The best-laid plans of mice and men often go awry." We all love when a plan comes together, and it all works out, but it is easy to become exasperated when projects do not work out. Have you noticed how easily some people can start assigning blame when that level of frustration is ramped up by a schedule?

GPS technology is impressive. However, have you ever missed a turn? My GPS will start recalculating to come up with an alternate route. You mean there's more than one way to get there? Sometimes before launching out on a trip, GPS will even provide a choice between the quickest route or a scenic route. In our busyness of living life, we seldom choose a scenic route. We make plans, and if those plans are altered, we become frustrated because for some reason, we miss a turn or there's traffic or road construction. We are all guilty of running about and feeling so important that we sound like the White Rabbit from *Alice in Wonderland*—"No time to say 'hello,' 'goodbye.' I'm late. I'm late. I'm late." Life is way too short to let uncontrollable circumstances give frustration the power to raise our blood pressure.

I imagine at the judgment seat of Christ, there will not be as much discussion about schedules as souls. You never know the blessings you rush past because you are more concerned about a plan than people. I've witnessed families have a knock-down-drag-out fight (in front of the pastor no less) because lunch wasn't on the table for the family gathering at the time announced. I've seen men lose their families because they were more concerned about making a living than loving their life. Working the plan is excellent, but make sure your plans are in keeping with God's plan for your life. Mark 8:36 says, *"For what shall it profit a man if he shall gain the whole world, and lose his own soul?"*

— ✣ —

My Story
Day 18

Trusting God...
in Exhaustion

But as for me, I shall sing of Your strength; Yes,
I shall joyfully sing of Your lovingkindness in
the morning, for You have been my stronghold
and a refuge in the day of my distress.

—Psalm 59:16

As the night rocked along, with a posse hot on the trail of the missing orders for the lumbar drain, the dreaded needle finally made its way into my room. Four must be a magical number for me. That is again how many attempts before an IV was started. Almost before my jaw relaxed from gritting my teeth, another needle arrived. A young lady from the lab came to draw blood. Doggone, if she did not stick me in the knuckle of my index finger on my right hand. Before this whole ordeal of "My Story" was over, I ended up with nine out of ten knuckles getting in on the fun. The news came that they had found the missing orders but to no avail. They couldn't place the lumbar drain yet because my blood was too thin. So they brought in two bags of blood platelets to thicken up my blood. I think it was either brown gravy or mud. Maybe platelets are the medical equivalent of "rubbing dirt on it?" It was cold running into my veins. Every hour, a different person from the lab showed up to thump around on my arms in search of a vein that would be a willing participant. Apparently, all my usable veins took refuge in and around the back of my hands. Finally, around 4:30 a.m. Saturday, it was decided that the lumbar drain was postponed. I went to sleep, counting pin cushions and porcupines. I rested for a solid hour.

There must have been some confusion about the whole postponement announcement because at 5:30 a.m., the young…very young doctor came in to insert the lumbar drain. The moon must have been in the seventh house and Jupiter aligned with Mars or the perfect storm was ending because they found the orders *and* my blood was thick enough to insert the drain. The young…very young doctor told me to turn on my right side. She explained this was similar to the epidurals my wife had received when our children were born. This information would have been helpful if she had not added a qualifying statement of "times ten." Wait. What? So I gritted my teeth again and watched the face of my wife who was peeking over watching the procedure.

The location of the bullseye was just north of my sacrum. A needle pierced through my skin in search of an entry place into my spine. Guess how many tries before successfully getting through at the right spot and into my spine? Yes, four! After the needle struck gold, a small catheter was inserted through the needle to travel into my spine and up above the leak. The purpose of the drain was to divert spinal fluid from above the leak to take the pressure off the location of the leak. Rerouting some of the spinal fluid would hopefully allow the dura to seal. It would also give my body time to absorb what had leaked out and was collecting in my back. As the needle sank deeper the fourth time, I prepared for a painful experience, but it truly was not unbearable. The young…very young doctor was now my hero. She had been a trooper all night coming in on the hour to facilitate the placement of the drain ASAP. I had high hopes that we had taken the first steps on the road to healing. Little did I know, this road led into a valley, and that valley had a shadow looming.

Our story: living by grace

In the 1964 stage musical *Fiddler on the Roof,* the milkman, Tevye, loves to try to quote the Bible. In one exchange, Tevye says, "As the good book says, 'When a poor man eats a chicken, one of them is sick.'"

Mendel challenges his Bible knowledge, "Where does it say that?"

Tevye's rebuttal is "Well, it doesn't say that exactly, but somewhere there is something about a chicken!"

We too allow statements that hang around long enough and maybe sound like they could perhaps be in the Bible to rise to the level of authority. One of those statements is "God will not put more on you than you can bear!" *But* that statement is *not* in the Bible. As a matter of fact, what the statement teaches is completely opposite of what the Bible does say. The Bible does say God does not tempt anyone Himself (James 1:13). The Bible does teach there is no *temptation* that God does not provide a way out of succumbing to do evil (1 Corinthians 10:13). God will provide a way out of temptation. However, God will also allow you to be placed under more difficulty than you can bear! The two, temptation and difficulty, are not the same thing.

The popular, but misguided thought is that difficulty is evil. Therefore, God doesn't intend for His children to endure difficulty. However, that is just not sound doctrine. There are some lessons we can only learn inside of difficult circumstances. Jeremiah was given a message as he watched at the potter's wheel in Jeremiah 18. God is the Potter. We are the clay in His hands. The wheel is the circumstances, the "turning" of life events. We are shaped by the pressure of the hands that mold us, but He uses the turning of life's circumstances to accomplish His design. I'm sure the clay feels the wheel is spinning around out of control. If it were not for the hands of the potter, the clay might go flying off the wheel when it turns so fast. The clay might rather sit there without spinning around and without any pressure. You know what happens to clay that sits there without the hands applying pressure and the spinning of the wheel? It gets dry and is not much more than a rock. If our lives are going to have shape and usefulness, then we have to trust our potter knows how to turn the wheel and shape us. Even after that, there's some fire involved too. Sometimes, God will turn up the heat to make something beautiful and useful out of us also!

There are times in our lives when we cannot see heaven quite so clearly as when we are on our back! There are times when we *must* come to the end of our rope, the end of strength, the end of resources, the end of our ideas, the end of our cunning, the end of our self, so that we will know, without a doubt, that God and God alone is the one to rescue us. Paul made it plain to the Corinthians that it was God and God alone who provided for him and saw him through everything he endured when he was in Asia. Second Corinthians 1:9–10 says,

> We were burdened excessively, beyond our strength, so that we despaired even of life; indeed, we had the sentence of death within ourselves so that we would not trust in ourselves, but in God who raises the dead; who delivered us from so great a peril of death, and will deliver us, He on whom we have set our hope. And He will yet deliver us.

When you are exhausted in life, He is our strong help!

— ❦ —

My Story

Day 19

Trusting God...in the Calm before the Storm

In the day of my trouble I shall call
upon You, For You will answer me.

—Psalm 86:7

MY HOPES OF THE LUMBAR DRAIN resolving my problem were growing fainter as the days grew shorter, or at least as the nights grew longer. Dr. Lovell and his staff continued to monitor my status almost hourly. It seemed they weren't any more optimistic than I. Finally, it was decided that I would be added to the surgery list for Tuesday, which also meant surgery would happen toward the end of the day as an "add-on." But hey, I was proud to make the team. I wanted to get back on the road to recovery. On the day of surgery, it was the same process that happened a few weeks earlier. After they rolled me out of the room, we all had the attitude of "been here done that before." I kissed my wife and said, "I'll see you in a couple of hours."

Since I already had an IV, the holding area was pretty relaxed. A standard blue bonnet was added to my attire. As the nurses and the surgery entourage came to transport me back to the OR, I told a funny story about my dad once being put to sleep, and instead of counting, they asked him to spell his last name. My daddy only got the first two letters out before he went to sleep. The funny part was my sweet innocent saint of a mother was the first one to catch on to what my dad had said, to which she responded, "I don't think I would have said that to a man with a knife in his hand." The entire staff laughed. I informed the nurse that I sometimes feel a little claustrophobic, so she held the mask at an angle. The last thing I remember saying was that I had prayed for every person in that room that morning. I wanted to pray with them now. The business of the room stilled, and I prayed a short prayer. I heard a sweet "thank you" from the anesthesia nurse holding the mask and from some others from different parts of the room. Then a gentle voice said, "You're going to go to sleep now." And I did.

Our story: living by grace

Warren Wiersbe made a statement that has helped me much in my walk of faith. In summary, he said life has many storms. Where you are in the experience of life is one of three locations. You are coming out of a storm where you testify of God's sustaining power or you are in the midst of a storm hanging on to your only hope or you are about to enter a storm. Enjoy the calm, but prepare yourself. The Bible gives us many warnings about always being ready and prepared. We are to suit up in spiritual armor prepared for battle (Ephesians 6:10). We are to stay alert because our enemy is a roaring lion (1 Peter 5:8). We are always to be ready to give a reason for the hope that is in us (1 Peter 3:15). We are to be prepared for our Lord may return like a thief in the night (1 Thessalonians 5:2).

My family and I lived on the Mississippi Gulf Coast for ten years. In our time there, a few hurricanes tracked through the Gulf of Mexico. Hurricanes Opal, Danny, and George were all closely watched and wreaked havoc just east of us. We lived a half mile north of the beach. We prepared for each storm by boarding up our windows. I sent my family north to stay with friends. The effects of each of the storms that hit while we live there paled compared to Camille of 1969 and Katrina in 2005. Some of the lifelong residents told the horror stories of Camille. We carried several work crews to help following Katrina. I found it fascinating to listen to those who were eyewitnesses to the events that made me shutter. All different and unique stories, but they all had one thing in common. Every one of their accounts described how, at the height of the display of the power of the storm, *they prayed*! It was the one common denominator I heard from all of them. From the most hardened, macho, tough guys and professionals trained to deal with traumatic events to the most petite, mild-mannered grandmother, they prayed!

When do you need to trust God more? The obvious answer might seem to be when you are in the middle of the storm. That is undoubtedly the most dangerous time and when it is most apparent, *or* is the answer after the storm is over? Everybody knows there's damage that needs to be cleaned up after a storm, and that is when a lot of injuries take place. Victims are emotionally tired, and they let their guard down, *or* maybe some would say you should trust God more before the storm because there is so much uncertainty and the need to ask for His protection and guidance. When do you need to trust God more? The answer is you need to trust God more in whatever moment you *are* right now. Thank God for what has passed, but you can't do anything about the past. You should trust God for what lies ahead. Our only certainty is that He is unchanging *"yesterday, today, and forever"* (Hebrews 13:8). But we are not promised tomorrow. It is futile to worry about that storm. You may not even be here to weather it. So glorify God Eternal. You should trust God more right now because right now is when we are least prepared, least hopeful, and most vulnerable. *If* you trust God right now, then you will never be unprepared, caught off guard, defenseless, off course, or vulnerable.

When Jesus walked on water, Peter asked to come to Him. If Jesus had been from Mississippi, He would have answered, "Well… y'all come on then!" Peter got out of the boat and walked on water. Peter, at that point in his life, there always seemed to be a "but." "*BUT when he looked at the wind and waves*," and he sank. The lesson to take away is, keep your eyes on Jesus! When? *Now*!

— ❖ —

My Story
Day 20

Trusting God...in the Storm

Though he slay me, yet will I trust in him.

—Job 13:15

FOR THE SAKE OF CONTINUITY, I will share the chronology of what happened in the next hours. I was present for every event, but I do not remember them, thank my gracious Lord! LeeAnn and her sister, Amy, were in the waiting room. I'm sure they were expecting in a couple of hours to hear a similar report they heard about five weeks earlier with the first go-around. After I was asleep, they rolled me over onto the operating table so I would be on my stomach. Dr. Lovell began the surgery by opening me back up and seeking to find the leak which was causing all the commotion. He reported later that every internal stitch from the former surgery had been broken. This would never have sealed spontaneously. He instructed the anesthesiologist to perform a technique that, in layman's terms, would give me a puff of air and elicit a response of a cough. The cough in turn would put pressure on the dura around my spine and help identify the exact location of the tear in the dura. At this point, things headed south.

The anesthesiologist warned the surgical team that I was in trouble. I was told later that they lost my pulse. Now one would think that the pulse is something you should keep up with. I mean, it's not like losing your keys or your glasses! I'm sure it was chaos in the operating room. There I was sprawled out on the operating table with a nine-inch incision wide open in my lower back, ruptured spinal cord exposed, lying on my stomach while my heart was trying to take his toys and go home.

One might think of the heart as the rich kid of your organs. The problem is when your heart tries to quit the game; he pretty much ruins the day for everyone else. When the heart leaves the game, it's his bat and ball with which everyone else depends to play. Dr. Lovell threw a few staples inside of my open incision and a long single-running stitch on the outside, just enough for a temporary hold. They turned me over onto my back. It is a funny thing when you threaten to rough up the rich kid who is trying to end the game and go home, then he'll usually come reluctantly back to play. When they turned me to my back, my heart repented and came back into the game. They found my pulse. I'm so glad it was not in my wife's purse!

In the urgency of that moment, they carried me to the cardiac cauterization lab, and apparently, my heart had a real temper tantrum there. He gathered up bat and ball and bases and all the gloves. He even scooped up the dirt on the infield and stomped off, heading to the house. I've heard Code Blue on TV, and a few times over hospital speakers. I did not hear this one, but it was happening all the same. When someone is in this state requiring a response to a Code Blue announcement, these trained professionals go into a different mode, a well-rehearsed plan to give that patient the best chance to live and recover. I was already intubated, which means they had previously backed a Ford F-150 up to me and inserted the tailpipe down my throat. That means they could help me breathe. Then they used a defibrillator machine. (This machine is not designed to render a person so that he will never be able to tell a lie…get it, defib). Instead, it delivers an electrical current to shock the heart, in the hopes of resuscitation. The first shock did not prevail. They up the amps and gave me the second shock. I'm glad my heart repented again and came back with bat and ball in hand to finish the game. However, did it have to use that bat to beat the stuffing out of me? But at least he brought the infield back and must have "rubbed some dirt on it" for my heart. It was later explained to me that a stent placed in the left anterior descending artery five years earlier had failed. I had a massive heart attack as a result. The artery is known in the medical field as the LAD, but to most of the world, it is known simply as the widow maker. The cardiologist ballooned the artery open and placed another stent. I hope it was a new and improved model.

Our story: living by grace

There are always documents to sign before any medical procedure. They tell you the risks associated with the procedure and then quote some inconsequential small percentage of the possibilities that anything can go awry. The person explaining never looks like they're trying to talk you out of the surgery. They cite the percentages of the risks more so to convince you to move forward. The look on their face could be compared with the attitude of a high school cheerleader's response when the class nerd asks her to the prom: "There ain't no way this is going to happen!" Hmm…but it can! Most people don't give this warning any consideration. But I do.

Before I have had any surgery or before I travel out of the country, I always make my wife have an unwanted conversation. It is reassuring to me to make certain she knows how much life insurance I have and who she would call about the financial and final arrangements, which I have already made. In the event of a tragedy, I want the easiest path for her to be able to put those kinds of things in motion without worries. I've got it all written down and in the safe. I make sure she knows how to open the safe. I'm prayed up, and I'm ready for *that* trip, the trip I won't have to pack a bag. There may be some of Paul's passages that I'd need to tweak or qualify or amend to make them fit my life exactly. However, there's one verse that I can say, "Yes, sir! Me too!" The passage is Philippians 1:21, "*For to me, to live is Christ and to die is gain.*" In other words, "if the Lord's got more for me to do here, then that's where you'll find me. If the Lord is ready to call me home, then that's even better for me, and that's where I will be!"

When you are flat on your back for more than a few hours, you are pointed in the right direction to make sure everything between you and God is right. Don't get me wrong; if I traced my steps to reconfess all of my sins, then I'd still be busy. But those are already settled. I've been forgiven, so I've spent the last days and weeks in some time in praise and gratitude. Flat on your back, especially the second go-around, will make you search your heart to make sure there's no unconfessed sin in your life. But after that, it's time to put it in God's hands. If you start asking why, then you won't get a satisfying answer, and you head off down a useless path. Believe me, I spent kidney stone numbers 2–118 there. It doesn't help. I finally have come to the conclusion that God is in control, and I'm not. *And* sometimes it's not about me. When you are in pain, that is a harsh reality. Pain makes you feel that everything is about you. But sometimes we're just the visual aid God is using to teach someone else a lesson in their life.

I never doubt God uses me when I preach, but that's not about me. I speak the message, but the Holy Spirit directs it into people's minds to bring conviction to their hearts, and they either follow Him or not. That's not on me. I just preach. I'm sure when I present the Gospel, God has to be the one to draw that person, convict them, and He's the one who saves them. It's not about me. I'm just the messenger. When I do some random act of kindness, then God speaks to people's hearts and uses the deed for His glory. That's not about me but what He wants to do with it. But when we suffer, it suddenly becomes all about me? No, let God use you where you are. Make sure your heart's right; and then show the joy of living, dying, and even suffering for the glory of God! That helps make sense of passages like 1 Peter 1:6–7.

In this you greatly rejoice, though now for a little while, if need be, you have been grieved by various trials, that the genuineness of your faith, being much more precious than gold that perishes, though it is tested by fire, may be found to praise, honor, and glory at the revelation of Jesus Christ.

My Story

Day 21

Trusting God...
Death Is His Call

But sanctify the Lord God in your hearts:
and be ready always to give an answer to
every man that asks you a reason of the hope
that is in you with meekness and fear.

—1 Peter 3:15

I WAS TAKEN TO THE INTENSIVE care unit; ICU was not about the gown now. My family was yet to discover the details of the big party that had just been held in my honor. They knew something was wrong, but they were led to believe it was a hiccup. (A side note: coughs and sneezes and hiccups played a much more important role in "My Story" than I ever intended)!

The day before had been my fifty-ninth birthday. According to the doctors and nurses, I came close to celebrating it with Judy. One doctor later pointed out to me that I had joined a very exclusive club: the Near-Death-Experience club. My reply was that I thought I was already a member because every time my dad took off his belt, or worse, sent me to cut my own switch, I thought it surely was a near-death experience.

People have asked if I saw a light or other loved ones or Jesus or what? Now in that condition of Code Blue, my heart stopped and shocked twice; and being told that I had come so close to leaving this world, you'd think my mind would seek comfort from some pleasant experience. Why didn't I see heaven? Why didn't I see the angels there to escort me into glory? At least, why can't I dream about sitting on Robert and Pam's porch in Wears Valley, Tennessee, watching the mist roll across the Smoky Mountains? Why can't I dream about walking along the beach at Grand Cayman holding hands with my wife? The only thing I remember experiencing was more like a dream. I was sitting in my office counseling two first-year college students and telling them there should be no rush to get married; how much easier life would be if they finished their education first! Really? Honestly, if I made a list of all my ministry responsibilities in the order I enjoy them, that kind of counseling would be toward the bottom of the list because it is so stressful.

I may not have had Paul's experience of seeing the third heaven, and I didn't see angels or see a bright light, but I did learn something when I woke up. God is still in control, and God is not finished with me here in this life. I don't understand why all this has happened to me, but I trust God does. It was not a scary reality when the medical staff said that I almost died, *but* I do not believe that it is precisely accurate. Please do not misunderstand; I know it was medically possible that I could have died and that everybody else that was in that room would agree with that assessment. However, that's not in my hands…nor was it entirely in their hands either. I am so grateful that they used all their knowledge and available technology to my physical advantage. I acknowledge that if they had *not*, then the result could have been very dire for me. However, I believe I'll live until God calls me home. God put the medical staff in that room and provided them to save my life; that was God at work, using people at work. I still do not know *when* death will come for me, but I trust that reality is contained in God's will and plan for my life, and not a moment sooner. Therefore, I long to be submissive to Him today.

I do not mean to give the impression that my attitude is that death is or will be welcome. No, death is still an enemy, but it has no sting. I do not look forward to the experience of death, but I do not dread the results of death.

Our story: living by grace

During his first year in college, a farmer's son returned home for the weekend and declared his faith was shaken. The farmer inquired as to why. The boy said that religion was just not logical, and he pointed to the pumpkins growing close by on the vines. He said it makes much more sense for the pumpkins to have the support of the great oak tree, while the vines seemed to be the logical choice to grow the tiny acorns. If there was a divine designer, wouldn't he know that? Suddenly, an acorn fell from the tree, hitting him on top of the head. His dad said, "Good thing it wasn't a pumpkin."

I do not have all the answers as to why things happen the way they do, but I'm confident that God does not make any mistakes. Job 42:1–6 records Job's confession, which humbles my heart: "*I know that You can do all things and that no purpose of Yours can be thwarted.... Therefore I have declared that which I did not understand, things too wonderful for me, which I did not know.... I have heard of You by the hearing of the ear, but now my eye sees You; Therefore I retract, and I repent in dust and ashes.*" There are some things that the heart can apprehend by faith, but the head just may not be able to comprehend or understand. In Matthew 19:26 Jesus said, "*With men, this is impossible, but with God, all things are possible.*" It is one thing to come to the reality that we don't understand all things, but it is another thing when we know that God does understand, and God is in control. It is a reality that sustains in this life...and beyond.

— ⚜ —

Day 22

Trusting God...with the Unseen and Unknown

For we know that if the earthly tent which is
our house is torn down, we have a building
from God, a house not made with hands,
eternal in the heavens. For indeed in this
house we groan, longing to be clothed with
our dwelling from heaven, inasmuch as we,
having put it on, will not be found naked. For
indeed while we are in this tent, we groan,
being burdened, because we do not want to
be unclothed but to be clothed, so that what
is mortal will be swallowed up by life.

—2 Corinthians 5:1–4

ALTHOUGH MY FAMILY DID NOT YET know the details about all I
was experiencing, they picked up that something was not going as
planned. When our children received that report, our oldest two,
Joshua and Emily, made arrangements to head to Memphis from
West Point and Shreveport, respectively. Our youngest daughter,
Abby, is a single mom and a school teacher in Hattiesburg, and she
couldn't come. Her older siblings assured her they'd keep her posted.

Joshua arrived that night and stayed with me in the ICU. LeeAnn and her sister Amy went to her dad's and spent the night. The doctors came in during the night and revealed to Joshua details of all that had happened. Joshua wisely waited until the next morning to tell his mama because she was already exhausted and upset. So he settled down in an uncomfortable chair and tried to sleep sitting up.

Joshua fell asleep and dreamed he was piloting a small airplane which suddenly started into a downward spiral with alarms sounding all around. He was awakened from his scary dream to a nightmare. They had me restrained to the bed with double restraints because of my size. I have always been strong and never afraid of hard work. Hauling pulpwood, bailing hay, wielding tread plate, and doing the physical labor expected of a grown man by the age of twelve helped develop within me a strong work ethic early. I lifted weights from my teenage years, off and on for most of my life. Thus, they should have used baling wire to restrain me, but I wasn't awake to tell them! I was still intubated and heavily sedated. The alarms Joshua heard were not from a dream, but they were literally sounding in the room.

I had managed to pull through the restraints and pulled out my own intubation tube. This is not a procedure I would recommend. When someone is intubated, there is a cuff built into the end of the tube that once in place, is inflated to hold the tube in your windpipe. When a doctor pulls the F-150 tailpipe tube out of your throat, he deflates the cuff, clears any mucus or debris, so it doesn't end up in your lungs. He puts some WD-40 on the tailpipe and slides it gently out of your throat. When you do it yourself, without deflating the cuff and no WD-40, then your endotracheal tube performs a Roto-Rooter from stem to stern, from can to can't. Within moments, the ICU room, which was not shaped like a triangle, by the way, was filled with people in white coats, scrubs, and an array of hats. Hey… why did I not get to choose the color of my bonnet?

Our story: living by grace

The Bible is filled with examples of ordinary people who couldn't see beyond their circumstances, but by faith, God gave them hope of something bigger than what they could see in front of them. Joseph was a shepherd who became a slave who became the second most powerful man in Egypt. Moses was a murderer who opposed Pharaoh and all of Egypt to redeem Israel. Gideon was a farmer who became Israel's judge. David was a shepherd who became king of Israel. None of these men could see the end in store, but they trusted God to use them. Second Chronicles 16:9 says, *"For the eyes of the LORD range throughout the earth to show Himself strong for those whose hearts are completely His."* When Abram left Ur, he knew God was leading him, but he didn't know where; he followed by faith one step at a time. The entire book of Hebrews gives example after example of how God has something better, but we must enter and follow His plan by faith. Hebrews 11 defines faith as *"the evidence of things not seen."* So the opposite of faith would be things we can see? Sometimes. We become experts. We begin to explain to God how life should go, how things get done, the way it ought to be. In Matthew 16:21–22, the Bible says, *"From that time Jesus began to show His disciples that He must go to Jerusalem, and suffer many things from the elders and chief priests and scribes, and be killed, and be raised on the third day. Peter took Him aside and began to rebuke Him, saying, 'God forbid it, Lord! This shall never happen to You.'"*

Peter could not explain the Transfiguration. He couldn't explain the giving of sight to the blind. He couldn't explain the calming of the storms; even though he had walked on water...still, he sank. But this uninformed Peter could "rebuke" Jesus? This is the loudmouth who dared to think he could tell Jesus "*this* is how it is gonna be!"

There is a difference between proclaiming loyalty and practicing loyalty. Peter was going to keep Jesus safe? Yet he couldn't even stay awake in the garden to pray! I'm glad God is always faithful. Joseph ran away from Potiphar's house naked and afraid, with no idea about all that God would do in his life. Moses stood at a burning bush with no idea of the magnitude of the assignment he was trying to talk God out of using him to accomplish. Peter cried when he heard a rooster crow, and he had no hope that God would ever do anything else in his life either. Faith is bigger and better because God is almighty to save!

— ⚜ —

My Story
Day 23

Trusting God...When You Don't Have a Clue

Hear, O Israel! The Lord is our God,
the Lord is one! You shall love the Lord
your God with all your heart and with
all your soul and with all your might.

—Deuteronomy 6:4–5

AFTER PERFORMING THE ROTO-ROOTER WITH THE intubation tube, I was fully awake. One of the men was trying to tie my right arm back down. I thought he wanted to arm wrestle. I was winning. If I did not have the end of that F-150 tailpipe and all that tape still in my mouth, I might have said, "Hey...you want to go left-handed now?"

Two voices were clearly alarmed and arguing at my right ear. One was saying that intubation had to be redone. She was yelling authoritatively, "We've got to get that tube back in!"

The other was yelling, "He's already got it out, and he's alert."

Although I still had a mouthful of the end of the tube and tape, I mumbled loudly, "It's out! It's out!" I'm sure I sounded like Frankenstein's monster, and if they had taken a peek under the covers and looked at my back at that moment, they might have believed I was him (or at least a Mel Brooke's version singing "Puttin' on the Ritz")!

The confusion stopped, and the voices calmed down. Someone removed the tape and began cleaning the bloody mess I made on my mouth, face, and neck. They asked me a variety of questions to see if I was completely alert, and I guess I passed. They untied my left hand. I felt a horrible stabbing pain in the side of my neck under my right ear. They told me it was a central line they placed in a hurry but instructed me to leave it alone. I'm sure they told me the same thing about the intubation tube too. I decided to abide by their recommendations to leave all other tubes, catheters, and needles alone. They all left my room, but I could hear them already begin the discussion for the next steps.

I lay there, assessing the situation. I knew where I was. I had an idea that something had gone very wrong while I was asleep but did not fully appreciate my circumstances. I remember praying with a sort of feeble weariness to say, "Lord, I trust you…and I'm glad you know what has happened because I don't have a clue…and I guess that's all I need to know for now." I think I even said that out loud.

Our story: living by grace

In Matthew 10, Jesus sends the twelve disciples out to heal the sick and cast out demons and preach the message "*The kingdom of heaven is at hand.*" Of course, there was an immediate and personal purpose that touched the lives of each person who heard their message and was helped by them. There was also a larger purpose for this mission. Jesus organized the logistics of sending them to assure these practical physical needs would be met before Jesus Himself reach these people with His message. This was a very practical ministry strategy. Jesus was truly a great man. Then Jesus shows the divine side of Himself with words about the future. He told the disciples the road ahead of them would be hard and gave them a glimpse into what their lives would be like after the Cross. They would be handed over to evil men, and they would suffer for the sake of the Gospel. Verses 19–20 say, "*But when they hand you over, do not worry about how or what you are to say; for it will be given you in that hour what you are to say. For it is not you who speak, but it is the Spirit of your Father*

89

who speaks in you." Jesus is not simply talking about persecution; He is teaching them a deeper lesson about God's character.

God is intimately involved, even when we are not aware of how He is working. God is paying attention to us even when we are not even conscious of His presence at the moment. God is loving you, even when you are at your lowest moment—God is there, and He is in control. Matthew 10:29–30 says, "*Are not two sparrows sold for a cent? And yet not one of them will fall to the ground apart from your Father. But the very hairs of your head are all numbered. So do not fear; you are more valuable than many sparrows.*"

Each of us moves through our day, and we do believe God is ever-present. Nonetheless, our limited focus is on work or reading or driving or conversing. However, when the fire alarms of life go off, then we want to *know* God is there. When you're standing in a Red Sea situation with the forces of this world bearing down upon you, you want to know there is someone who is able to part the waters. When you're standing in the fiery furnace of life, you want to know the fourth man is standing with you to not only keep you safe in the furnace but deliver you out. We soon discover He is even able to keep you from smelling like smoke! When the sun rises on the dead army of Sennacherib, which numbered 185,000, we'd probably all agree that it is good to know even one angel. However, it's best to know the one whom angels serve! We all acknowledge the hand of God in our everyday life when we skid on the ice but miss the other cars. We know it's the working of God when we code on the operating table and live to write about it. *But* do not miss the ever-present hand of God who also is involved when you comb your hair in the morning. He not only knows if the number of hairs on your head has decreased; He knows *which hair* is in the comb. There are situations like in that ICU room when I may not fully comprehend or even have a clue about the details of what has happened around me, but it is a great comfort to know our God is sovereign and personally at work and in control!

— ❧ —

My Story

Day 24

Trusting God...There's Always One

That I may know Him, and the power of
His resurrection and the fellowship of His
sufferings, being conformed to His death.

—Philippians 3:10

AFTER THE INITIAL EXODUS OF THE medical folks left my room to go check their own blood pressure, Joshua stepped up to my bedside. I didn't even realize he was there. To see his face was such a comfort. He reported to me all that had happened. It was a little more than my rattled mind could grasp. We talked for a while. He sat back down, and we both drifted off for a nap, I think.

I woke up to someone standing beside my bed calling my name. It was the anesthesiology nurse, or maybe she was a resident doctor. She was the young lady who had held the mask at an angle in the operating room so I wouldn't get claustrophobic; the sweet girl who laughed at my awkward joke, calming my nervous energy; the kind eyes for whom I had prayed; and the last voice I heard as I was put to sleep. She was now standing beside my bed. It was then I recognized it also was the same voice that was my advocate to confirm my intubation tube was already out earlier.

This young lady had come back into my room alone, and it didn't seem she had a medical task to perform. She became emotional as she spoke. She said, "Mr. Funderburg, I sure am glad to see you awake because you almost left us."

My immediate reply was not preconceived. It was simply my response. "Well, apparently, God is not finished with me here yet. He's got more for me to do."

Her lips quivered, and she said, "I'll never forget the prayer you prayed in the OR. I've never had anyone do that before. It was so genuine."

My answer again was as honest as I could say it because I believe it. "Oh, it's not about the pray-er—the one saying the prayer. It is about the one I was praying to. I know Him personally. How about you?"

She patted my hand and shook her head in agreement. She said, "I am a believer, but I've allowed my faith to be shaken. Tonight was a wake-up call for me."

It was a meaningful moment. This single encounter has helped me to partly define what I had experienced, or at least maybe why.

Our story: living by grace

"There's always one!" I've heard that statement, and not always with a hopeful outcome for me. Those are not the words any kid wants to hear sitting in the principal's office or standing in the hall with a teacher and maybe especially in the pastor's study. Yes, I was that kid. I didn't get in trouble often, but when I did...as I said before, Funderburgs go big, or we go home. However, I've also been singled out when it was a good thing. I won an essay writing contest for the local newspaper once. I was nine, and the prize was an electric razor. It would be another two years before I even had peach fuzz. I won a bench press contest. I won best actor of the year in both high school and college—an ability that would have helped earlier in the principal's office if I had only known.

There have been a couple of other times when I needed to stand alone, or so I thought, decisions I had to make alone. The night I was saved, I thought it something I had to do alone. When I finally surrendered to Christ, I found out I wasn't really looking for Jesus; He was looking for me. In Luke 15:4–6, Jesus said:

> *What man among you, if he has a hundred sheep and has lost one of them, does not leave the ninety-nine in the open pasture and go after the one which is lost until he finds it? When he has found it, he lays it on his shoulders, rejoicing. And when he comes home, he calls together his friends and his neighbors, saying to them, "Rejoice with me, for I have found my sheep which was lost!"*

There are times when I've been preaching, I can tell there's that one person who is dealing with some internal struggle as if he or she is the only one in the room. I've seen the response of the white knuckles holding on to the pew in front of them, and with the closing prayer, they hit the door faster than a deacon who needs a cigarette. But I've also seen people respond that I realize didn't personally need me, but I just happened to be the one to tell them the Good News. I've seen the response of that person who couldn't wait for the music to start for the invitational hymn. I'm a big man, but I've been bear-hugged at the altar by a sixty-year-old ninety-pound woman that almost knocked me off my feet. I've witnessed God move the heart of people in my office, outside in parking lots, with a man dressed "in drag" on a street corner in New Orleans, in jail cells, in homes, in my home, at the cemetery, during wedding counseling, in hospital rooms. Once I went into the wrong hospital room and was apologetically excusing myself when I was convicted that it may not have been a mistake but instead may have been a divine appointment. I stuck my head back in the door and was a bit nervous about how to advance the conversation when the man asked me, "Are you a pastor? Do you have just a minute? I need to talk to somebody." It thrills my soul to witness people hearing the Gospel one at a time. We can make it seem so difficult as if only pastors or deacons can share the Gospel. I would say God seeks out and saves people in spite of pastors and deacons.

I've been around church and church culture long enough to know we can get the cart before the horse. We want to seek out great numbers of people, but that's not how any of us were saved. We were saved in the simplest of terms, one at a time.

A man was hiking through part of Europe. As he approached a small village, he saw an old man sitting on the porch, leaning against the wall smoking a pipe. The hiker approached the man and asked, "Were there any famous men born in this village?"

The old man studied the question, drew on his pipe, and said, "No…no famous men. Only babies."

The birth of every baby happens one at a time. So it is being born again. That too happens one at a time. Every day we should seek the chance to share the Gospel simply. There's always one!

— ❧ —

My Story
Day 25

Trusting God...
Agreement in Prayer

Therefore, confess your sins to one another,
and pray for one another so that you
may be healed. The effective prayer of a
righteous man can accomplish much.

—James 5:16

I KNOW THROUGH MY ENTIRE ORDEAL, the word spread via text messages, phone calls, social media, and maybe pony express and carrier pigeons to share how desperately my family and I needed the prayers of the saints. I know God doesn't get confused, but I've been called a lot of different names in my lifetime, a few I'll not share. Every name that was called out in prayer must have registered. There were folks who prayed for Dale, Daddy, Papa, Brother Dale, Pastor, Dale Pete, Big Bird, Hoss, Reverend, and even Perry to the official world. All those prayers benefited me in my most desperate time. I'm most thankful that God not only knows my name, but He knows my heart. Honestly, when I woke up and learned of all that happened, I had a calm peace that overshadowed me. That peace was not found in my own confidence; it was a peace that surpassed understanding.

Over the minutes and hours to follow, friends from West Point came to comfort my family. My sister Donna came to lay eyes on me, to both comfort my family and seek comfort herself, and to make sure I was going to be all right. LeeAnn's youngest sister, Brandi, came to hold my hand and shine her smile on me and comfort her sisters. Phone calls and messages from all over the world poured into my family. I am truly a blessed man by no other means than God's grace and God's gracious people.

Methodist Hospital is a teaching hospital as well as a first-rate health care facility. As I lay in the ICU, flat on my back with the sound of monitors and the busyness of the staff, I saw the cardiologist with a group of about ten young doctors in tow enter the unit. I heard them stop at the two rooms to the east of my room. I listened to him tell about the patient, their condition, and then ask questions. The young doctors would answer and then pose their own questions. They would have a discussion about what could have, should have, would have happened if different factors were presented. It was quite interesting...until they stood outside my doors.

I heard the doctor tell the unvarnished version of the patient's circumstances and condition. As I heard him describe it in no uncertain terms, I began to think about the poor fellow he was describing and thought, *Man, I need to pray for that guy.* Then it dawned on me; I am that guy! After much discussion about what they made sound so terrible and almost unbelievable it could unfold the way they said, the teaching doctor asked, "What if the neurosurgeon had not stopped when he did?"

One of the students replied, "The patient would not have made it."

That was alarming enough, but another student doctor said, almost under his breath, "He actually should not have made it anyway."

In reaction, I raised my head and voice and said, "Haven't any of y'all heard of prayer?"

I'm not sure what looks came across their faces because I couldn't see them. But they got really quiet and still. In just a few seconds, they softly moved to the next patient.

Our story: living by grace

I enjoy watching college football. There is one element that I believe is getting out of hand in football because it is out of hand in our society in general. The self-gratification and celebration after the completion of every play have gotten entirely too elaborate. Defensive linemen are in the game to tackle. Receivers are in the game to catch the pass when it is delivered. The prancing, chest-beating, taunting for doing your job seems distracting and arrogant. What if after cashing a check at your local bank, the teller shouted and danced around her chair? What if after leading a church family in a powerful singing of "How Great Thou Art," the music minister spiked the hymnal? And when God answers our prayers or uses us to share the Gospel or allows us to be the hands of Jesus "to the least of these," then why should we feel anything other than faith, gratitude, and awe of God alone? The only confidence it should provide should be directed to Him and our place found *in* Him. It should be as natural as a child crawling up in the lap of his Papa and feeling loved and safe and accepted. First John 3:1 says, *"See how great a love the Father has bestowed on us, that we would be called children of God."* Now that's a truth that fills my heart with love, security, and acceptance.

Why would the great sovereign God even hear my prayer, much less answer my prayer? If you listen to some TV preachers, you'd think God's sole purpose is to wait on them to give Him a suggestion. Their description sounds like God should slide down the chimney with a bag of riches to award them with prosperity because He is impressed with them. Some of them are so impressed with themselves, I can't believe they don't have continual shoulder trouble for patting themselves on the back for impressing God! Everything about each of our lives has a purpose—and that is to glorify God! We seek His will as the desires of our heart, not the other way around. Psalm 37:4 says, *"Delight yourself in the Lord; And He will give you the desires of your heart."* If the desire of your heart springs from delighting in the Lord, then *His* glory is paramount. John 14:13 says, *"Whatever you ask in*

My name, that will I do, SO THAT *the Father may be glorified in the Son.*" God answers prayer, not so we can look at others and say "Neener-neener!" but so that we can look to the Father and say, "Praise Jesus!"

My Story

Day 26

Trusting God...and the People He Has Gifted

Now there are varieties of gifts, but the same
Spirit. And there are varieties of ministries,
and the same Lord. There are varieties of
effects, but the same God who works all things
in all persons. But to each one is given the
manifestation of the Spirit for the common
good. For to one is given the word of wisdom
through the Spirit, and to another the word
of knowledge according to the same Spirit;
to another faith by the same Spirit, and to
another gifts of healing by the one Spirit.

—1 Corinthians 12:4–9

THERE WAS AN ARGUMENT THAT ENSUED over the next few hours between the cardiologists and the neurosurgeons. I still had the lumbar drain. My back was still considered an open incision with just enough staples and stitches to keep me from bleeding out. They said there was a high risk of infection. There was still a surgery to be finished. They had me on a particular medicine to keep my blood thin enough because my heart had attacked me and for the sake of the stent. I believe the medical name for it was super-duper-high-dollar turpentine, but I could be mistaken. The benefit of this particular blood thinner was that the properties make it possible so that the effects of the drug could be out of my system within forty minutes. Theoretically, they could halt this medication with no worries about me bleeding to death during the spinal surgery and without compromising my heart condition or new stent. The rub was they only had three bags of the medicine, not only in the Methodist Hospital but in all of Memphis, in all the mid-south. Don't I feel special!

I already received one bag, and the second was half-full, or half-empty, considering your disposition. The other issue was the lumbar drain. The cardiologist insisted that the drain had to go because of the blood thinner. The neurosurgeons declared "Not over my dead body." Oops...wait...unfortunate hyperbole, but you get the point. They said no, the lumbar drain stays. I thought, *I'll let them duke it out.* My money was on Dr. Lovell though. The compromise was to cut the rate of the "turpentine." This decision would make it last until the next day, which by now was Thursday. The drain stayed.

Our story: living by grace

Any believer who studies the Bible knows the story of Nehemiah. What he is best known for is his leadership to return to Jerusalem to rebuild the walls after years in exile. Can you even imagine the logistical nightmare of traveling so far, gathering needed timbers and materials to rebuild the defenses of Jerusalem? The Bible tells us; also, he had to deal with the resistance and mockery of Sanballat, Tobiah, Geshem, and company. It is an incredible story. But the beginning of the story for Nehemiah did not start as a construction supervisor or motivational speaker or military genius. He began as the cupbearer of the most powerful man in the world at that time, King Artaxerxes of Persia. It was a trusted position. It led to an apparent friendship, but one of great respect. The king observed Nehemiah's sadness and inquired about the reason. That may seem like an obvious expectation in our modern sophistication, but it was not in the ancient Persian culture. If the cupbearer showed anything other than submission to the king, it would have meant his life. There was little reason for eye contact, much less a bad mood in the presence of the king. God used Nehemiah, and we know about his accomplishments to reestablish Jerusalem through faith. *But* God also used the influence of the Persian king. Nehemiah prayed about what he was to do. Nehemiah put actions and words to those prayers to seek the help of one who had the power and influence and resources to accomplish his purpose.

There are times God has a purpose He intends to use you to accomplish, but that does not mean faith in God excludes everybody else. God heals our bodies, but He uses doctors and nurses and researchers just like he used the king of Persia. God provides for our needs, but we cannot limit how or who God may use to do so. Along the way, He may use the most desperate of circumstances also to use you in their lives too. I am convinced that there are people in our path that need to see Christians, not in the victorious praise of hands held high to worship God, but they need to see our struggle. They need to see our hands held up in surrender. They need to hear that we don't have it all figured out, but we trust God anyway! Until the world sees us striving to give Jesus the battle of our everyday flesh, then some of them will never have hope beyond themselves. We can't be all smiles all the time. There needs to be a saltiness in our lives.

The world needs to see, even when we stand in the "valley of the shadow," that it is as real to us as it is to them; but we are not afraid because we do not stand alone. Hebrews 11 defines faith as "substance" and "evidence" even when it's "hoped for" and "unseen." Matthew 5:13–16 says:

> *You are the salt of the earth; but if the salt loses its flavor, how shall it be seasoned? It is then good for nothing but to be thrown out and trampled underfoot by men. You are the light of the world. A city that is set on a hill cannot be hidden. Nor do they light a lamp and put it under a basket, but on a lampstand, and it gives light to all who are in the house. Let your light so shine before men, that they may see your good works and glorify your Father in heaven.*

My Story

Day 27

Trusting God...Certainty in Uncertain Times

Why are you in despair, O my soul? And
why have you become disturbed within
me? Hope in God, for I shall again praise
Him for the help of His presence.

—Psalm 42:5

ON THURSDAY, THEY CAME TO ROLL me down what was becoming a far-too-familiar hallway. You could tell my "bed driver" had a hidden desire to be in NASCAR. He navigated the halls so that I looked up once to see if we were drafting in the slipstream of Dale Earnhardt Jr. at the Brickyard 400. We must have been the lead car, but I couldn't see behind us. We slid into the OR, and the pit crew was there, but not to change tires. They made arrangements to accurately establish the lumbar drain apparatus. If you've ever been in an operating room before they put you to sleep, you need to be quiet because you might awaken the polar bear in the corner; the place is cold.

Before you receive sedation, you will notice some very casual conversations between the staff. The operating room is their office, their work environment, their water cooler. As they lay out the tools of their trade, everybody knows what they're doing, but it's a day in the office for them. Every once in a while, somebody will say something to the patient, and sometimes they seem a little surprised when you give a reasonable response. As I said, I have a high tolerance to pain and a high resistance to medication. The normal "goofy" shot is either of no effect upon me, or maybe I'm goofy enough all the time that no one notices. But when I took the initiative of that moment and ask again if it would be okay with everyone if I pray with them, all the noise stopped suddenly. I think some of them had been in this same situation about thirty-six hours earlier and maybe thought I was giving myself last rites or something. After I prayed, the noise of preparation started back up, but not the conversations. Everyone in the room knew what had happened the last time we all were here.

It was not my intention to make anyone uncomfortable by praying, so I said, "Hey, guys, it's going to be all right!"

I felt someone squeeze my foot and say, "Yes, it is! It's going to be okay."

A few seconds later, another hand touched my thigh and said, "You're going to be all right!"

Another few seconds and the familiar eyes stood to my left with a mask in hand again and said, "You're in good hands."

I shook my head and said, "Either way!"

She held the mask at an angle, and soon I felt warmth going into the vein in my arm, and the lights went out again.

Our story: living by grace

My mother was a godly woman. As I previously and painfully shared, her last few years were challenging, not only because of the decline of her physical health but far worse because of her mental state. She had dementia. Dementia and other diseases like Alzheimer's rob their victims of memories, their perception of reality and, eventually, even change their personality. It is a cruel and devastating progress to witness. There were days when my mama didn't know who I was and other days when she thought I was her brother or her daddy and others when she thought I was *my* daddy, her husband; and wow...she was mad at him vicariously through me. But there were a few days in the early stages when Mama would be clear and would realize that she was not well. She would tell me on those days that when the time came when she might not know what was best for herself that she trusted me to make the right decisions for her well-being. I tried my best to do just that. Those were some of the most challenging days of my life. When Mama was at her worst, there was still something deep inside that she knew she could trust me. She may not be able to call my name, she may not remember just exactly who I was, but Mama knew she was safe.

Some experiences of this life defy our ability to explain or understand. Some tests come to our faith when we cannot give a reasonable argument for why we hold on to God. However, we hold on, but not because our confidence is grounded in our ability to hold on to Him. Our confidence is in His ability to hold on to us. He doesn't lose his grip, even when we lose our grounding in spiritual reality, forget our spiritual identity, becoming confused and disoriented. The truth is that on our best days, it was never really about us! The object of our faith is Christ (Ephesians 2:8–9). The confidence that we can have abundant life is found in Him (John 10:10). It is the same confidence that keeps abundant life and everlasting life and eternal life always bound together. Life in Christ is about His grace to forgive us and change our destiny for eternity. It is based upon His ability, His character, His grace that benefits us in this life and the next. Second Timothy 1:12 says, *"I know whom I have believed, and am convinced that he is able to guard what I have entrusted to him until that day."* When life or death or eternity becomes more than you know how to make sense of it all, then enjoy the peace of knowing who stands guard for you.

—— ⚜ ——

My Story

Day 28

Trusting God...with a New Reality

I have been young and now I am old, Yet
I have not seen the righteous forsaken
or his descendants begging bread.

—Psalm 37:25

I WAS PUT TO SLEEP...AGAIN, AND the surgery was completed without any issues—no "Funderburg factor" this time! I was moved to the ICU step-down unit and laid flat for another forty-eight hours—easy peasy! The next days of recovery were a little more difficult the second time around. My body had endured a lot. I now understand why they call it a massive heart attack. For the first few days, I was secretly nervous because at times, it felt almost like I was hyperventilating; but the annoying probe taped to my finger said my oxygen saturation rate was in the high 90s percentile. There was a sensation that I can only describe as a flutter in my chest. However, my blood pressure was excellent. I would almost experience those feelings associated with claustrophobia, a little bit of panic when my heart would flutter, but then it would settle down and go away.

I was on a continuous EKG, with the electrodes in place. I innocently and mistakenly called these electrodes pasties once, which in turn caused all the women in the room to snicker. I only did that once. I would later learn some ill-witted Nazi designed the adhesives on the electrodes to contain super glue. The nurses reassured me that all of those flutters and feelings dealing with my heart would settle down in days or a few weeks. My floor nurses were the first ones to say to me, "You've got to be patient. Your body has endured a lot. You need to give it time to heal and catch up." But they weren't the last to express these warnings.

In ancient cultures, as a returning conqueror would approach his home city, there was a runner ahead of him to tell the citizens he was near. It served the purpose of the announcement so the city would be ready to receive him appropriately. I'm pretty sure there is a runner just ahead of me, both physically and electronically, bearing the news that I am approaching and needing a good lecture on the values of patience in healing. I've heard that message at least half a zillion times either face-to-face, by phone, by text, or by other social media. I not only heard it from nurses but from every doctor I've talked with since my heart "showed out," as my grandpa would have described it. I've had surgery before. I've heard that statement about patience during recovery before. However, this is the first time in which that prideful little voice has not whispered internally, *Oh, in a couple of weeks, I'll be fine.* This time, maybe I needed a good lecture. I now agreed with the warnings because my body seemed to be telling me it was right. My spirit was warning me that if I pushed too much, too soon, then it could result in being too late and too far, if there even was a next time. I would not likely be in the heart cath-lab next time. Now that is a sobering truth. The double whammy was my spinal cord. The dura is paper-thin. Mine had been cut open to remove the tumor, sealed, and then ruptured and sealed again in the same area. I could not risk doing anything to jeopardize another rupture. I would not survive.

Considering I had been put to sleep four times within five weeks, with three of those times within forty-eight hours of each other, the message was clear. My blood had been drawn the other half a zillion times. An IV was placed in at least a dozen locations. I was cut open three times all the way down to the white meat, my spinal cord cut open twice, and nerves shoved around like shoppers at Walmart at a Black Friday sale; my heart had attacked me while it was having a disagreement with the doctors. The doctors retaliated and shot enough electrical current through my body to qualify for at least a few steps with Tom Hanks down *The Green Mile.* There was also enough medication pumped into my body to fuel the truck that I felt must have run over me. I got the message. I'm fifty-nine, not nineteen. The days of picking up the rear of small cars are over. Now I was more concerned about picking up my rear and going home.

Our story: living by grace

Baptists talk a lot about grace. Reformed theologians speak a lot about faith. There is no doubt when we must connect the truth of grace and faith to any discussion of salvation. Ephesians 2:8–9 are Bible verses considered as staples for our spiritual diet: *"For by grace are you saved through faith; and that not of yourselves: it is the gift of God: Not of works, lest any man should boast."* However, once we move past the understanding of our salvation, I have discovered there are many believers that develop a strange sense of our own righteousness. It is a warped view that somehow after being saved, then it is sort of up to us and our ability to walk with God as if our *sanctification* was any less the work of grace as our *justification.* Please do not misunderstand; I wholeheartedly believe we should make real-time and conscious decisions about obedience and the surrender involved in discipleship. However, the power to do so is also found in grace through faith. Do not be guilty of cherry-picking Bible verses at the neglect of context. Ephesians 2:8–9 are connected to verse 10 also, which says, *"For we are his workmanship, created in Christ Jesus unto good works, which God hath before ordained that we should walk in them."* We are not saved *because* we perform "good works," but we perform good works because we are saved!

Physical health is undoubtedly affected by lifestyle choices. However, there are also genetic factors that make us who we are too. I did not choose my height or frame, but I do decide what I put on that frame. I will never weigh 210 pounds (as BMI charts suggest for a male who stands five feet seventeen inches). But I don't have to weigh 340 pounds either. I am given the undeserved gift of faith to be saved, and I have been saved to walk accordingly. The power to do so comes by the same power whereby I've been saved. I cannot boast in my own strength about it either! Oh, the vast complexity of the truth of God's grace.

— ✤ —

My Story

Day 29

Trusting God...when Life May Not Be Easy

Let me come back to where I started—and don't hold it against me if I continue to sound a little foolish. Or if you'd rather, just accept that I am a fool and let me rant on a little. I didn't learn this kind of talk from Christ. Oh, no, it's a bad habit I picked up from the three-ring preachers that are so popular these days. Since you sit there in the judgment seat observing all these shenanigans, you can afford to humor an occasional fool who happens along...If I have to "brag" about myself, I'll brag about the humiliations that make me like Jesus.

—2 Corinthians 11:16–18, 30
(The Message)

THE PASSAGE ABOVE IS A QUOTE from The Message translation of the Bible. Although The Message pushes the edges of the meaning of the original language into a flavor of American vernacular, it nails the passage in 2 Corinthians 11 spot-on and clear. It is the most honest rant you will read from Paul. The verses I did not print between verses 18–29 is actually the plain truth about all of the hardships Paul endured. However, Paul felt a little "foolish" and awkward sharing these experiences, but they were helpful for the church to understand the message and the man behind the message. I feel the same awkwardness about this part of "My Story," but my purpose is the same—to make clear this part of my reality. However, the following discussion causes me to be much more vulnerable and transparent than I am comfortable in writing, but as Paul said, *"Don't hold it against me if I continue to sound a little foolish. Or if you'd rather, just accept that I am a fool and let me rant on a little."*

In the past, I have had other health problems. My daddy was considered a classic stone former, thus his CB radio handle was Kidney Stone. Even after he advanced to the ham radio world, there were still people that knew him as Kidney Stone. My handle was Mongo from a character on *Blazing Saddles*, if that tells you anything about my teenage years. My dad also had heart problems. Before I graduated high school, my dad had thirteen heart attacks. He developed diabetes around the age of sixty. People often tell me how much I look like my daddy. Well, I'm sorry to say our medical records have a few elements that resemble them too. I have experienced 220 kidney stone attacks to date. My dad had his first stone at twenty-seven years old. I was twenty-seven when I had my first stone. I participated in a study in 1993 at Oshners Hospital in New Orleans. I was classified—you've got it—a classic stone former. I seem to be predisposed to other health issues that are notorious with Funderburg genetics too. However, over thirty-seven years as a pastor, I've only missed three Sunday mornings because of kidney stones. I've preached some of my best sermons when having a kidney stone, but I hope I never have another one. I've had heart issues for years, starting with high blood pressure since I was a child. Other health situations not related to genetics have been thorns in my flesh. I was hit by a car in 2014, which broke my back at L3. The surgeon placed pedicle screws and rods during a fusion surgery. I was back in the pulpit in two weeks. I had hernia repair more than once. I was back in the pulpit in two weeks. My return was not out of pride but because I felt good and ready to return! These recent experiences of "My Story" has been most challenging, and even weeks after returning home, I still felt as if I had been run over by a…wait! Bad analogy. Let me just say; I didn't feel I was progressing as well as I hoped.

Our story: living by grace

In John 4, we find the story of Jesus's journey through Samaria and an encounter known as the woman at the well. Knowledge of ancient near-eastern culture helps one understand that her trip to the well for water in the middle of the day is a clue that she has problems. The conversation with Jesus reveals some deep-seated pain of her past. There was some built-in hurt just because of the historical conflict between Jews and Samaritans. The Jews looked down on them as half-breeds after the return from Babylonian exile. There was long-term hatred on both sides. Culturally, there was gender prejudice of the day that even made the conversation with Jesus, a man, unlikely. She had trouble with Judaism. She had a problem with men. She had been married five times and was in an inappropriate relationship with a different man at the time. She was a troubled soul. She had trouble with relationships, but the answer to all of her pain could only be found in a new relationship with Christ.

Life is simply not fair. Our culture places barriers to the pursuit of anything righteous from the beginning. Our personal guilt is evident in our fleshly desires that lead away from God. When challenging circumstances explode on the scene, it becomes very easy to believe we are victims. As victims, we look to place blame everywhere except where it belongs. Our hearts become crowded with excuses rather than honesty. Repentance is not only feeling wrong about our past, but it is a change in the way we think and understand. Repentance is not only a change in behavior but a different way of thinking. It is not merely turning over a new leaf. It is climbing down out of the tree! It owns the accountability for our own sin, but it recognizes the grace of God as the only acceptable atonement through Christ's death, burial, and resurrection to provide our forgiveness. Second Corinthians 5:21 says, "*For he hath made him to be sin for us, who knew no sin; that we might be made the righteousness of God in him.*"

111

When our health is complicated, it becomes easy to allow the echoes of that old *victim mentality* to become the loudest voice. That voice continues to tell us that life should be "fair." We begin to ask the question of why. If you allow yourself to listen, that will become the loudest noise in your heart. Don't do it! Second Corinthians 10:4–5 says, *"For the weapons of our warfare are not carnal but mighty in God for pulling down strongholds, casting down arguments and every high thing that exalts itself against the knowledge of God, bringing every thought into captivity to the obedience of Christ."* When difficulty comes, and that old carnal victimized mindset raises the question, then bring it captive with your own question of "Why *not?*" God is more interested in building my character than in providing my comfort. If He can serve a higher purpose through hardship than comfortable circumstances, then to God be the glory!

Day 30

Trusting God...with the Rest of My Story

For this reason I also suffer these things,
but I am not ashamed; for I know whom
I have believed and I am convinced
that He is able to guard what I have
entrusted to Him until that day.

—2 Timothy 1:12

I WAS VERY THANKFUL FOR BEING discharged from the hospital and able to go home before Thanksgiving. I needed to be with my family. I referenced the *Wizard of Oz* earlier not as an authority in my theological training, but still, Dorothy said it well, "There's no place like home." That statement is especially true after you've pulled back the curtain and realize there's no wizard back there that's calling the shots or can damage you. My God is almighty to save.

People have been so kind, but people are curious. People have expressed they want to know how this whole experience has "changed" me? I do not believe the experience has actually changed me, but it has confirmed me. Everything I believed about God, about death, about heaven, and about eternity has not changed. It has confirmed how precious my family is to me. It has confirmed how blessed I am.

It has confirmed how I love my church family. It has confirmed the Word of God. It has confirmed me in my faith, not change it. Will I live differently? I hope so but by the same standard as any follower wanting to be conformed to the image of Christ should always want to live. Will I preach differently? I hope not because I've always stood on the Bible. Will I dread walking back through that valley of the shadow in the future when my days are complete? I will not dread it because I don't dread it now. I hope this experience makes me more patient, kinder, more compassionate, more forgiving, more convicted, more passionate. However, those are all the traits, attitudes, and actions for which I pray God to work in me on the most boring days of my life. The experience I have shared as "My Story" has called into focus just how frail I am, which in turn makes me lean on Jesus more. That cannot be a bad thing. Every time I cough, I think I'll remember how frail I am, and it will remind me how great my God truly is. Every time I sneeze or hear anyone else sneeze, I will know just how pure and powerful it is to say "God bless you."

Our story: living by grace

Over the last one hundred years, technology and equipment have been invented and developed to make our lives more productive and more comfortable. We've come a long way from a handwritten letter that may take months to arrive on foreign soil to talking to each other around the world in real time. One hundred years ago, there were no computers, no smartphones, no internet, not even television. As each of these inventions came on the scene, I'm sure each was billed as the best thing since "sliced bread." But one hundred years ago, there wasn't sliced bread! That didn't happen until Otto Frederick Rohwedder invented his Kleen Maid Sliced Bread machine in 1928 at the Chillicothe Baking Company in Missouri. A lot of things have changed in a short time. Sometimes people express how quickly change happens with the statement "It can happen in a heartbeat." Well, a lot can happen without a heartbeat too! A family is changed forever when a doctor does not bring a good report. A company can go from profitable earnings to bankruptcy with a wrong investment. A country can be turned on its heels in an election cycle. A lapse of judgment can ruin a reputation.

But the counterpoint is that life can be changed for eternity by repentance and belief too. It may feel like it happens in a moment. However, God has worked behind the scenes atoning for sin, to draw and convict each person and save us since *"before the foundations of this world"* (Ephesians 1:4). As we struggle to live in the moment and walk by faith and faithfully as believers, God empowers and gifts us to serve Him and His purpose. We all have failures and moments of regret. The words of Paul fit fresh on the lips of us all, maybe every day we live, *"Oh, wretched man that I am"* (Romans 7:24). However, we pick up the pieces and have to agree with God to live victoriously. We can waste our lives while being defeated or victims or self-indulgent, or we can reach forward and press toward why we are born and why we are still here. God has more…always more, so in the words of Philippians 3:13–14, *"Brethren, I count not myself to have apprehended: but this one thing I do, forgetting those things which are behind, and reaching forth unto those things which are before, I press toward the mark for the prize of the high calling of God in Christ Jesus."*

— ❦ —

My Story Is Our Story

Day 31

One More Day

And he said unto me, My grace is sufficient
for thee: for my strength is made perfect
in weakness. Most gladly therefore will
I rather glory in my infirmities, that the
power of Christ may rest upon me.

—2 Corinthians 12:9

GRACE ABOUNDS...

As I shared in the opening pages, I started writing "My Story" as a therapeutic exercise at the suggestion of a speech therapist at the Methodist Hospital. The idea to divide this and use it as a devotional guide meant an opportunity to tie thirty devotions, encased in biblical principles as "Our Story." Biblical principles crossover and have an application into every believer's life, regardless of circumstances, time, or age. I made it through "My Story" because I believed the truths found in "Our Story." A month's worth of devotions, but some months have thirty-one days! I would have been just fine with thirty. However, the Lord added one more day. So if this one is for you, then I hope you see God's hand in it. Colossians 1:24 says, *"Now I rejoice in my sufferings for your sake, and in my flesh, I do my share on behalf of His body, which is the church."*

Just a little more than two weeks after arriving home from the hospital, again I was amazed at how slowly my strength was returning. I do not mean to seem impatient with grace or ungrateful for healing, but I'm just being honest; I expected to be feeling much better. But I didn't. I was well beyond the point of feeling trapped indoors; I longed to leave the house. However, when I would try to push myself a little more physically, then taking a shower and getting dressed would utterly deplete my energy reserve. I looked forward to sitting on my back porch, but I still could barely sit through a cup of coffee. My blood pressure was fluctuating. It would drop out of the bottom sometimes at night. It was still a little high in the middle of the day. There was just no rhyme, nor reason to it. Then on December 11, 2019, I woke up a little earlier than usual. I didn't feel particularly well, but nothing overwhelmingly alarming either. I had my quiet time, fixed myself some coffee, and watch the news for a little while. Watching the news these days can make anyone feel bad, so I'll blame it on that. I wonder, *Will Donald Trump be blamed for what happened next because it seems he's getting blamed for everything else.*

I felt odd. My son is a band director and was a percussion major in college. So I've heard enough drum rudiments to know my heart was playing a double paradiddle pattern inside my chest. It turns out my heart is a pretty good drummer. I tried to check my blood pressure, but my cuff kept displaying an error symbol. I found myself hovering over the toilet with my face in a place not made for my face. My wife was telling me she was calling 9-1-1. Between bouts of throwing up, I was protesting, "No, really…I think I'll be okay… barf…really…barf…I'll be okay!" Macho will kill you and is often confused with stupidity. I was demonstrating both.

Thankfully, LeeAnn is neither macho nor stupid. She called 9-1-1. West Point Rescue Unit was at my house in a matter of minutes. I know all these men. They are always the epitome of professionalism. They had aspirin and nitroglycerin in me in between the blue bags for me to call "Ralph" a number of times and had me loaded up and headed to the hospital quicker than a Baptist preacher can inhaul a chicken wing at Sunday dinner.

As I arrived at the ER, my family doctor and the ER staff were there waiting on me. An IV was started on the second try. My heart rate was over 200 beats per minute. So they gave me a "goofy" shot, and while I was checked out, they shocked my heart. Within minutes, I was heading for the helicopter pad. They were having trouble loading the board on which I was strapped, so I told them if they'd let me get up, I'd be more than happy to help them out. They declined. They knew I would have run away. I also asked, if they didn't mind, "Let's fly by the church and see about scaring off the buzzard which is rousting in the nearby tower." But they declined that request too.

We landed at North Mississippi Medical Center in Tupelo about twenty minutes later. I was carried to the CPC—the chest pain center. The cardiologist that consulted me was not my regular cardiologist, but I had met him several times before. He told me that there was an issue with the circuitry of my heart, and he would perform a cardiac ablation that would correct the problem. I was carried to the lab where this procedure is performed, and I was prepared. They again put a central line in my neck below my right ear and then placed needles with a diagnostic catheter in both sides of my groin, and soon after that, I was put to sleep. The next thing I knew, I was back in the room with my wife, sister Donna, nephew Andy, Glen, and John from our church. I would have to stay to make sure the bleeding from all the entry points was sealed up without issue. We left the hospital around 4:15 a.m. My heart rate was normal, but I felt anything but normal. It was a very long day.

Psalm 90:12 says, "*So teach us to number our days, that we may apply our hearts unto wisdom.*" I do not know the actual count for the remaining number of days in my life. But I know who does know. I actually have no determinative factor over that, but I can apply my heart unto wisdom and live out what time God has ordained for me to love Him and serve Him with all I have and in all I do. I rest in the simple truth that I am in Christ and He is in me, and that is an eternal love that nothing can separate neither in this life nor in death. One day, "My Story" will come to its conclusion in this life, and they will place a date on a headstone at a grave in Monroe County. But I am glad to know *His* story in me will never end. "Our

Story" will go on. Another man who encountered much more than I was Job. Job's words are more fitting to express our faith beyond the moment and beyond this mortal experience: *"For I know that my redeemer liveth, and that he shall stand at the latter day upon the earth: And though after my skin worms destroy this body, yet in my flesh shall I see God: Whom I shall see for myself, and mine eyes shall behold, and not another"* (Job 19:25–27).

About the Author

DALE FUNDERBURG GREW UP IN RURAL Mississippi where life revolved around faith, family, friends, and community. Dale grew up in a Christian home in Amory with his parents and two sisters. Dale was fortunate to be influenced early in life by his godly grandfather, faithful pastors and ministers of music and youth ministers at his home church of FBC Amory, and all of his teachers and coaches.

Dale received his education through the Amory school system, Blue Mountain College, and New Orleans Baptist Theological Seminary. Dale has pastored Baptist churches across the state of Mississippi for more than forty years. He is presently the longest-tenured pastor of First Baptist Church in West Point, Mississippi. Dale has led revivals and mission teams to make Christ known from New York to Florida, from New Orleans to Indiana, from Wyoming to Arizona. Dale has taught and preached worldwide, including in China, Russia, the Philippines, Honduras, and Guatemala.

Dale is blessed to be married to his sweetheart of more than forty years, LeeAnn. They have three married children—Joshua (Lacy), Emily (Chris), Abby (Jessie)—and four grandsons: Elijah, Jack, Luke, and Elliot.